Birds&Blooms
Ultimate Guide to Birding

House wren,
page 169

Table *of* Contents

4 INTRODUCTION

6 CHAPTER ONE
Basics of Bird-Watching

38 CHAPTER TWO
*Create a Bird-
Friendly Habitat*

68 CHAPTER THREE
Feeding 101

98 CHAPTER FOUR
Gardening for Birds

132 CHAPTER FIVE
Common Backyard Birds

170 CHAPTER SIX
Birds In-Depth

204 CHAPTER SEVEN
*Birding Beyond
Your Backyard*

230 CHAPTER EIGHT
Ask the Experts

252 RESOURCES

ON THE FRONT COVER
*Black-crested titmouse,
photo by Alan Murphy/
BIA/Minden Pictures*

Eastern phoebe, page 11

Introduction

Attracting birds to your backyard just got a little easier. The *Ultimate Guide to Birding,* brought to you by the editors of *Birds & Blooms* magazine, shows you how! Filled with expert ideas for creating your own bustling bird haven, it shows the top foods preferred by your favorite winged visitors, how to create a safe environment they'll want to nest in and the very best plants you can grow to keep them coming back.

Get identification tips for common backyard birds. Learn more about the secret life of birds, such as where they sleep. Plus, plan your next trip to a bird-watching hot spot with travel info and insights for locations around the country.

We hope the advice in these pages inspires you to go on nature-themed adventures and to share your love of birds with family and friends.

—The editors of Birds & Blooms *magazine*

Anna's hummingbird, page 202

ASSOCIATE CREATIVE DIRECTOR:
Christina Spalatin

DEPUTY EDITOR:
Kirsten Sweet

ART DIRECTOR:
Sharon Nelson

ASSOCIATE EDITOR:
Julie Kuczynski

CONTRIBUTING LAYOUT DESIGNER: Jennifer Ruetz

COPY EDITOR:
Chris McLaughlin

PRODUCTION ARTIST:
Jill Banks

SENIOR RIGHTS ASSOCIATE: Jill Godsey

Contributors

Sheryl DeVore, George Harrison, Kenn and Kimberly Kaufman, Ken Keffer, Heather Lamb, Rachael Liska, David Mizejewski, Melinda Myers, Kelsey Roseth, Sally Roth, Anne Schmauss, David Shaw, Deb Wiley

© 2019 RDA Enthusiast Brands, LLC.
1610 N. 2nd St., Suite 102, Milwaukee, WI 53212-3906

International Standard Book Number:
978-1-61765-916-4
(Hardcover)
978-1-61765-883-9
(Paperback)
Library of Congress Control Number:
2019945277

Component Number:
118500053H

CHAPTER 1

Basics of Bird-Watching

From how to identify bird songs to pro tips for taking the perfect picture, get started on the fun!

Year-Round Guide to Watching Birds

The best tips for enjoying your favorite feathered friends in every season.

SEASONALITY IS A STRANGE THING. Those of us who live far from the equator integrate the seasons into our lives quite naturally. We are always aware of the change of the seasons—the shifts in light and temperature, the changes in the trees, flowers and crops in our gardens. For birders, these changes are even more dramatic, as each season brings its regular species, highlights and, yes, even periods of the doldrums.

Birds adjust not only their plumage, behavior and food based on the seasons, but they also make mind-bending migrations across continents and oceans in response to them. These movements and behaviors add a dimension to the year-round changes for those of us who watch birds. Each season brings something new, something different, something that demands that we sit up and pay attention.

Waiting to be Surprised

Winter can seem dark, cold and lifeless. Those of us who live in the northern part of the country (very far north in my case of Fairbanks, Alaska) are accustomed to snow, frigid temperatures and a landscape that can seem void of any living thing. From a birding perspective it can be monotonous. Common feeder birds flit in and out, the same few species, day in and day out. We long for the days of spring and summer.

But then, during one of our periodic glances out the window, something different appears: a pine grosbeak, perhaps, a northern shrike or a red-breasted nuthatch. The new bird flies into the branches, scattering a flurry of snow as it lands. The colors and patterns of the new arrival help us forget about the cold, the dark and the monochromatic landscape. We become entranced by the bird at hand.

This is winter birding for me in the interior of Alaska, but a similar story can be told virtually anywhere. In western Washington state, where I attended college, winter was one of the finest times of year for birding as species from across the North congregated in the wetlands and estuaries. And although there was far more diversity in those wet coastal forests than here in Alaska, one trait remained constant: Things often seemed the same, day after day.

Rain there, snow here. The species were usually the same, though there were far more of them. But the rarities and the surprises served to remind me that despite the apparent monotony, things were not always the same after all.

Try to Keep Up

The pleasures of watching birds really come to light during the changes of the seasons. Wherever you live in North America, the appearance of the first migrants is a cause for celebration. It is a sign that winter has lost its grip and the warmth of spring is not far away.

Every spring day is a bit like Christmas because there is bound to be a new gift waiting, if one is willing to look for it. In the South, the first signs of spring may not be the arrival of a new species but the sudden absence of the winter residents. Meanwhile, farther north we wait for the arrival of those same species: snow buntings,

Red-breasted
nuthatch

juncos, longspurs or robins. Spring is a fleeting time of sudden and constant change. It forces our attention, incites the desire to step outside, to listen and to watch.

Spring is also a time of sudden and ephemeral abundance. Weather patterns and migration occasionally coincide to create what are known as "fall-outs." Like construction on an interstate, bad weather can create a traffic jam of sorts along the migration route. Countless birds can be caught up behind the storms, waiting for their chance to move north once again. This phenomenon is particularly dramatic along the Gulf of Mexico and the Great Lakes, where flocks of migrants sometimes descend from the sky, decorating the shrubs and trees like colorful, living ornaments.

Migration, of course, is not always so dramatic. Often it is as simple as backyards, recently silent, newly filled with the sounds of birds. Not all species arrive at the same time. The sparrows are often first, heralding the arrival of others. Birds arrive one species after another until the last wave of wings has flowed north up the continent.

Flurry of Activity

When the blasts of heat arrive with summer, the birds change their tunes. They, like us, settle into a routine. Summer, so different from winter in many respects, surprisingly bears some similarities.

It can be a time of apparent stagnation. But unlike the cold months, it is the stagnation of a tropical lake—still, yes, but filled with expanding life as nests are constructed, eggs laid and

WEATHER PATTERNS

Weather plays a large role in bird activity. If a storm comes through, it can affect birds for thousands of miles. Left, American robins often travel together in winter because it's easier to find food. Below is a robin's nest hidden among spring azalea blooms, and at right is an eastern phoebe in summer.

hatched, nestlings fed and eventually fledged. The species may not change all that much, but the birds are boisterous and multiplying.

The mottled browns and streaky plumage of the first juvenile sparrows challenge the identification skills of the most astute birder. Then as observers get a grasp on the sparrows, fledgling warblers and flycatchers appear, and the challenge begins anew. Confusing us more, adult birds look worn and tattered, like the tired parents they are, and seem to sulk in the brush, exhausted. For a few weeks in July and August the trees are again filled, as fledglings disperse and adults start to fuel up for the molt into their winter plumage and the migration to follow.

One day in September a species or two goes missing. Like partygoers who attend out of politeness or obligation, the last species to arrive is often the first to leave. Here in Alaska, the alder flycatcher, a species that spends only around 6 weeks on the breeding grounds, is the first to

flee the North and start its journey to the far southern portion of South America. Soon another species follows, then another and another.

By early September in my neck of the woods, there is a veritable flurry of fluttering wings as one after another the migrants pick up and fly south, the first tendrils of winter brushing their retreating tails. As winter again grabs control of the landscape, left behind is a small cluster of resident birds breathing a sigh of relief as they reclaim the forests, fields and backyard feeders as their own.

—*David Shaw*

Attract Birds in Every Season

Eastern
bluebird

Birdhouse
in redbud

WINTER

- Add an electric de-icer to your birdbath, or buy a birdbath with a built-in heater. Birds need water every day, even when it's cold out.

- Notice robins and bluebirds that stick around in cold and snow. These birds don't always head south in winter. But their habits may change—they often travel in flocks this time of year.

- Brush snow and ice off your feeders and your flowers, and keep berry bushes clear. Birds are most vulnerable after a snowstorm or ice storm. You can also use part of your cleared driveway for ground feeding, so juncos can easily find their millet.

- Look for irruptions of birds, by species that suddenly show up where they're not usually seen in winter. Flocks of evening grosbeaks, pine siskins, redpolls and crossbills often do this.

SPRING

- Make sure your birdhouses are ready to go. Bluebirds are among the earliest nesters. They use man-made housing and like it facing open fields. Mount the proper house about 5 feet high on a pole, and keep an eye on it to make sure house sparrows don't move in.

- Use cling decals on your windows to keep spring migrants from crashing into the glass. In spring and fall, more birds are on the move, making them more likely to die from run-ins with windows.

- Remember that not all birdhouses are suited for your favorite fliers. Find our birdhouse guidelines on page 252, or check with a local backyard-bird store to find out which houses are suitable for your resident birds.

- Offer birds nesting materials, such as string, yarn and hair. Put these in a mesh bag or an empty suet cage—the birds will love it.

Juvenile
seaside
sparrow

American
goldfinch

DAVE WELLING; WILLIAM LEAMAN/ALAMY

SUMMER

- Learn how to tell if you're seeing a juvenile bird. By the time young birds leave the nest, they're almost as big as their parents. So watch for clues—such as youngsters flapping their wings begging for food or looking rumpled as their feathers grow in.

- Go on a nest hunt. See if you can spot a few nests hidden in the trees and shrubs.

- Don't assume young birds on the ground have been abandoned. In most cases, they don't need your help at all. They've probably just left the nest, and the parents aren't far away.

- Keep an eye out for warblers and other fliers as they begin to head south for winter. Migration isn't just a fall phenomenon. It starts in late summer. Remember that not all birds will be in their typical spring plumage. Challenge yourself to identify the mystery fliers you see.

AUTUMN

- Don't forget to look for goldfinches. Even though they lose their familiar gold coloring in fall and winter, they're still out there looking for seed, such as thistle.

- Watch for flickers eating ants and towhees searching for decaying matter before the ground freezes.

- Pay close attention to juncos. Their arrival in fall marks the transition from warm to cool weather. Dark-eyed juncos have white bellies, which you rarely see because they eat on the ground. Try to glimpse a flash of pure white before they fly away.

- Keep track of your backyard visitors by writing them down. You can track patterns and behavior. Birds are creatures of habit. Next fall, you'll have an even better idea of what you'll see and when you'll see it.

Northern mockingbird

Bucket-Seat *Birding*

Don't try it while driving—but if you're in the passenger seat, here's how to spot birds from the car.

Snowy owl

BIRD-WATCHING IS AN APPEALING HOBBY because you can do it anywhere and you don't need special equipment. In fact, one of my favorite birding destinations isn't a destination at all. As long as I'm a passenger, I love birding on the open road.

I'm especially fond of back seat or shotgun-seat birding in winter. You can cover some diverse areas in a hurry, and when you find birds, you've also got a built-in blind—and a heated blind, at that! So hop in the car, truck or van and let's go find some birds.

Farm Fields

Farmers' fields are expansive and look quite barren in the winter, but on closer inspection you'll usually spot thriving birdlife. Scanning the field with your binoculars will often reveal flocks of horned larks flashing black tail feathers that contrast with their light bodies. Occasionally you might find a pipit or a longspur flying along, too.

In cold weather, two unique snowbirds can sometimes be spotted in these plowed fields. Strikingly patterned flocks of snow buntings can be seen as far south as the plains of Colorado. And if you ever think you see a plastic grocery bag hung up on some corn stubble, look twice: There just might be a snowy owl looking back at you.

Black-billed magpie

Prairies and Grasslands

I have a little confession to make: I sometimes do some birding even when I'm driving. (No, I am not recommending this!) For me, western road trips aren't measured in miles but in black-billed magpies and American kestrels perched along the way.

I grew up in northern Wyoming, where the first sign of winter wasn't a snowflake. It was the first rough-legged hawk that I'd spot from Interstate 90.

You can often see raptors soaring high above the roadway, or those and other birds perched along fences and electric lines. Take a look along your drive, but don't fret if you can't always identify the birds. When you're in the driver's seat, it's better to focus on the 18-wheelers zooming past than on even the most intriguing bird.

Deserts

One of the most memorable bird encounters of my life happened while I was in my car. The first roadrunner I ever saw was perched in a tree. From there, it glided down and ran along the road right beside my vehicle.

Another bird to look for along desert roadsides is Gambel's quail, which will often scurry along the side of the road, too.

And it's not just birds you'll spot when you get off the beaten path. Look for javelina (similar to pigs, but in the desert), lizards and other critters. You can often get a better look at them along the road than when hiking.

Wetlands

Cattail marshes and open water are easy to scan from your vehicle. I've been known to stand on the door frame of my little car to get a better view of the scene. It's easy to get a panoramic view that lets you scope out blackbirds, ducks, herons and more. You might even spot a rail slinking along the shoreline.

Many National Wildlife Refuges have begun to embrace the concept of car birding. Auto tour routes are often near wetlands and can provide access to parts of the preserve that are more sensitive to human encroachment. Having visitors stay in their cars can minimize the disturbance. Car routes are also ideal for folks with limited mobility.

Shorelines

While summers at the coast are crammed with sunbathers, winters are packed with birds. I've spent many days car birding on the Ocean City, Maryland, inlet, where I marveled at the birds as the winter winds whipped and the surf pounded. The bobbing of brant, scoters, scaup and long-tailed ducks in the waves nearly made me seasick, but I stayed as cozy as could be in my truck.

Bird-watching on the shores of Lake Erie and Lake Michigan has always reminded me of oceanfront birding. So many species of gulls show up in the winter that I'm always thumbing through my field guide trying to ID them. This is something I'd be far less cheerful about doing if I didn't have a cup holder for my coffee or if my fingers were numb from the windchill.

Snow buntings

Great blue heron

IT'S EASY to get a panoramic view that lets you scope out blackbirds, ducks, herons and more.

Gambel's quail

Parking Lots

It's true, many lots attract a limited variety of species, mostly gulls and house sparrows. But there are some real gems in surprising locations. Even if you're just at the supermarket, get in the habit of taking a quick look around before you jump out of the car. You'll be rewarded with birds that you'd miss otherwise.

Parking lots in rest areas can be real treasures. Often planted with the only trees for miles around, they provide shade for weary travelers as well as shelter for birds. Even a quick stop can give an exciting snapshot of the species of the region.

From city parks to backcountry byways, your vehicle can provide a bit of comfort and shelter for your next birding experience. You can pass the time by watching for birds while you zoom by, or you can get up close as you use the car as a mobile bird blind. Either way, you'll be rewarded with great birding on the go.
—*Ken Keffer*

Greater
roadrunner

Virginia rail

THE ROAD GOES ON FOREVER

Car birding can be easier than exploring on foot. Here are a few ways to get involved in conservation efforts without ever leaving your vehicle.

BIRDATHONS

These fundraising events rely heavily on car birding. To get thorough coverage, teams usually take to the road for at least part of the day. Look for one in your area.

BIG DAYS

Big Day bird count efforts are designed to maximize coverage and minimize wasted time. Routes are meticulously planned, and truly hard-core teams barely slow down as they cross species off their day lists.

BIRDING TRAILS

Pioneered in Texas in the mid-'90s, birding trails are catching on around the country. These designated byways connect networks of birding hot spots. The roadways themselves often are as rich with birds as the parks and nature centers they connect.

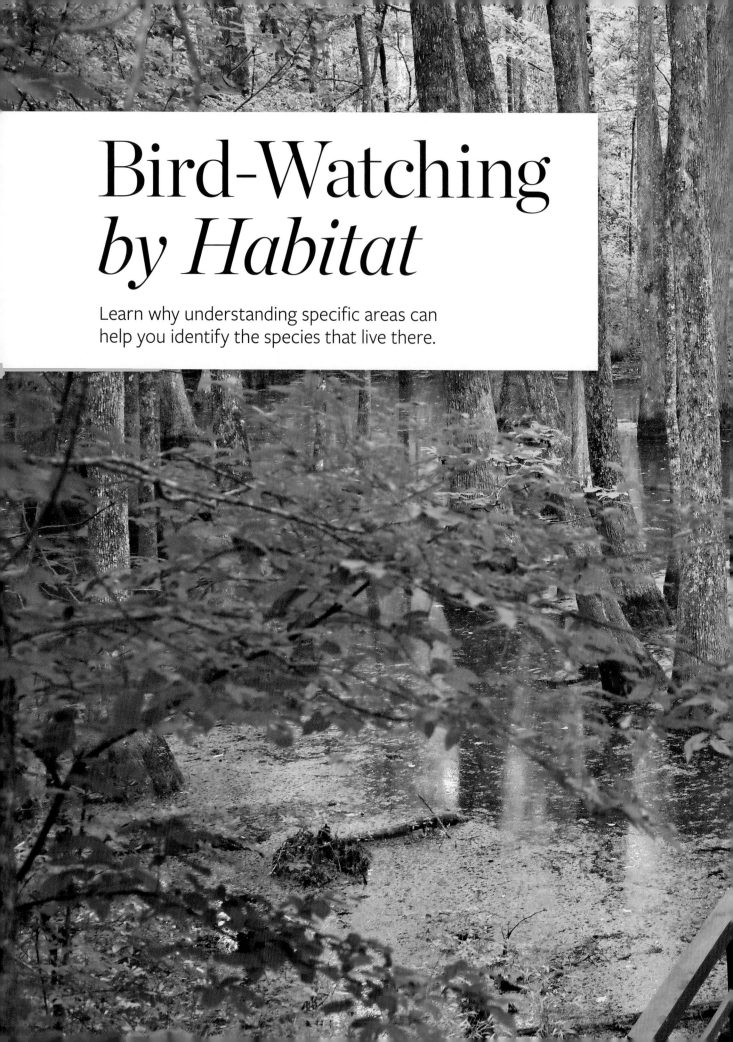

Bird-Watching
by Habitat

Learn why understanding specific areas can help you identify the species that live there.

DID YOU KNOW?

The boardwalk trail at Cypress Swamp allows you to walk above a water tupelo and bald cypress swamp at Natchez Trace Parkway near Canton, Mississippi.

Great blue herons will pause in Florida wetlands.

YOU CAN MAKE a connection between birding and everyday activities. Take shopping: Have you ever thought about how going in search of particular items at a shopping center is like bird-watching? To find what you're looking for, you have to go to the right store. To buy a book, you go to the bookstore. To buy jewelry, you go to the jewelry store.

Birding is similar, because every kind of bird has its own preferred habitat. The prothonotary warbler likes swamps, so you wouldn't look for one out in the desert. The American pipit lives in wide-open spaces, so you wouldn't expect to find one in the middle of a dense forest. Learning about the habitat preferences of various birds can help you find different species in particular places, and help to identify the ones that you find.

Killdeers will nest in vacant lots.

Recognizing Different Habitats

Of course, in the shopping center, most stores have signs out front, making them easy to recognize. Natural habitats don't always have signs posted, so we have to identify them for ourselves. Here are a few examples of fine bird habitats.

FOREST OR WOODLAND: This is the most widespread habitat in North America, but there are many different kinds of forests, each with its own typical birdlife. The birds in a spruce forest usually will be different from those in a forest dominated by oaks and hickories. A typical forest usually has several layers, including a canopy and an understory of lower vegetation, and different birds can be found in these different tiers. A few of the many birds that call the forest home are the red-shouldered hawk, pileated woodpecker, yellow-throated vireo, eastern screech-owl and wood thrush.

WETLANDS: Bogs, fens, marshes and swamps are all wetland habitats. Wetlands, which support aquatic plants, are essential habitat for many wonderful, often elusive birds. Birds commonly found in wetlands include the iconic great blue heron, the secretive sora, swamp sparrows, red-winged blackbirds and common yellowthroats.

GRASSLANDS OR PRAIRIE: A field of grass might not seem like the best place for birds to raise young, but many species build their nests very low, or even on the ground. Many of our favorite birds rely on grasslands for nesting, and because this habitat is disappearing, some of these species are declining in numbers. Let's hope that more people will understand the value of grasslands to birds like the bobolink, meadowlark, dickcissel, greater prairie-chicken and Henslow's sparrow.

SCRUB-SHRUB: At first glance, scrub-shrub habitat might not look like much. Characterized by low shrubs, short trees and other woody plants, scrub-shrub looks like a forest that failed. Lack of understanding and appreciation of its value has led to a serious loss of this important habitat. Yellow-breasted chats, Florida scrub-jays, field sparrows and blue-winged warblers are just a few of the birds that rely on scrub-shrub to build their nests and to raise young.

VACANT LOT: A vacant lot is habitat? You bet! For some birds, every scrap of habitat matters. We have seen killdeers in more open lots and gray catbirds in shrubby ones. Some housing developments in Florida even have burrowing owls nesting in vacant lots.

BACKYARD: Your yard is automatically going to be a habitat of some kind, and if you think about providing shelter, food and water, it could accommodate many birds! Some of the species that move into backyards readily include eastern bluebirds, chipping sparrows, northern cardinals and mourning doves.

Pileated woodpeckers prefer forests.

Florida scrub-jays like scrub-shrub.

Using Habitat to Recognize Birds

An awareness of habitat doesn't just help with finding birds—it helps us identify them, too. For example, several kinds of small flycatchers look very much alike, but tend to have different haunts. Willow flycatchers are usually found in scrub-shrub thickets or in willow groves along streams. Least flycatchers prefer edges of woods or old orchards, while Acadian flycatchers are found deep inside swamps. These habitat clues are often easier to discern than any field mark.

Paying attention to habitat can even help with the challenge of recognizing birds by sound. Chipping sparrows, swamp sparrows, pine warblers, worm-eating warblers and dark-eyed juncos all sound similar, singing a simple, dry trill. But their habitat preferences can help tease out who's doing the singing and turn a challenge into a "trilling" experience!

The chipping sparrow is a common backyard bird for many people because it likes the semi-open habitat of suburbs and farmyards. But what if you hear a similar song coming from the middle of a marsh? Chances

are you're hearing a swamp sparrow. If the song is coming from the treetops in a grove of pines, the bird may be a pine warbler, but if you hear it from near the ground on a hillside in dense woods, it could be a worm-eating warbler. And if it comes from treetops in a cool, moist evergreen forest, you may be hearing a dark-eyed junco. Even the most experienced birders use habitat clues to help them identify bird voices.

Now you know how learning bird habitats can help you. But increasing your awareness and understanding of habitats can help birds, too. The more we understand the habitat preferences of different species, the better equipped we are to protect these areas and the birds that depend on them for survival.

Black
oystercatcher

Horned
lark

8 BIRDS AND
THEIR HABITATS

*No two species have exactly the
same habitat preference. Here
are a few examples of birds and
their favorite hangouts.*

HORNED LARK. Wide-open spaces, like
plowed fields, beaches, tundra, desert,
plus airports and other short-grass areas.

COMMON LOON. In summer, northern
ponds surrounded by evergreen forest.
In winter, open ocean bays or large lakes.

SUMMER TANAGER. Forests of oak and
pine in the Southeast, cottonwood groves
along rivers in the Southwest.

CACTUS WREN. Mostly desert areas.
Locally, also in dry, brushy woods.

BLACK OYSTERCATCHER. A shorebird
that avoids sandy shores; spends its time
on rocks pounded by waves.

HOODED WARBLER. Understory of rich,
moist woods, edges of swamps.

BALTIMORE ORIOLE. Edges of deciduous
forest, open groves, parks and towns with
lots of shade trees.

WOOD DUCK. Swamps, rivers, ponds
surrounded by tall trees.

A chickadee's most common call sounds like it's saying its own name, *chickadee-dee-dee.*

Tune In to *Songs*

Whether protecting their territory or finding a partner, birds create fascinating music for all kinds of reasons.

FROM LOVELY MELODIES to raucous squawks, birds make all sorts of interesting sounds. Of course they aren't making that variety of sounds just to entertain you; they have more practical reasons for belting their hearts out. Birds use songs and calls to communicate with other birds, particularly their own kind, and when you dig deeper, the reasons get even more complex.

A few species, such as turkey vultures, are almost always silent, but most birds are chatterboxes and have several different calls. This is especially true for birds that live in flocks for part of the year, such as chickadees.

Black-capped chickadees have at least 15 distinct calls that they use in different situations. If their flock is foraging in treetops, they make short, light "contact" calls, but a louder note when the flock is set to move on. Chickadees make various alarm calls when danger is near. Rival males have aggressive calls they use when they're about to have a showdown. Members of a mated pair have several noises they use to communicate with each other near the nest, and young chickadees make food-begging and distress calls.

Some types of alarm notes are recognized by other birds, not just the species that makes them. When a mixed flock of different species is moving through the forest and one member spots an approaching hawk, it pays for every bird in the flock to recognize the alarm call.

While calls typically consist of a single note, bird songs tend to be more complicated and have a very distinct purpose. The songs can be beautiful, like those of the wood thrush or hermit thrush, but that's not always the case. The yellow-headed

A yellow warbler is caught in midsong.

Male Baltimore orioles sing to defend territory or to lure a mate.

VOICE LESSONS

Birds generally are born knowing how to make the right call notes by instinct, but many have to learn their songs by listening to adults of their own kind. For that reason, some species (like white-crowned sparrows) have song "dialects" that vary from one place to another, while the calls tend to be the same within every location.

blackbird, for example, has a rough nasal snarl for a song. But although it's not the prettiest song out there, that harsh performance works just as well as any of the other more melodious offerings from different bird species.

Primarily the male birds sing, mostly in the breeding season, and they use their songs to announce a territory claim. If you see a male robin or oriole singing away, he's warning other males that this plot of ground is already taken and to stay off his turf. His song can also serve to attract a female or to help the male stay in touch with his mate, but territorial defense seems to be the main motivation.

However, the male in some warbler species has two song types: one for chasing away other males and the other for keeping in contact with his mate.

And there are some bird species, especially in the tropics, in which the males and females even sing duets. All of these different sounds add variety to nature's soundtrack.

Chestnut-sided
warblers spend
their winters in
Central America,
often joining up
with flocks of
tropical birds.

Follow the Owls

Be a bird sleuth and discover who's flying through the neighborhood. Watch for these telltale signs.

IF YOU'VE NEVER seen an owl in your backyard, that doesn't mean one isn't there. These mysterious birds are nocturnal predators, so they hunt in the darkness after you've gone to bed. Their special feathers allow them to fly in complete silence, making them even more difficult to hear than they are to spot. Put on your detective's cap and become a sharp-eyed owl observer.

Look for Clues

To spot an owl, stay up late and do some nocturnal wildlife-watching from the comfort of your deck or on your next camping trip. As human activity dies down for the evening and the smaller animals that owls prey on become active, you are more likely to spot one of these nighttime birds.

Binoculars are a must for owl observation, and if you're a birder, you probably have a set handy. If you don't own a pair yet, there are plenty of high-quality, beginner binoculars to get you started.

Thanks to excellent camouflage, owls are still able to fly under the radar once the sun comes up. If you move quietly and scan patiently, you may be able to spot an owl on its daytime roost. Owls often roost in dense evergreens. They'll also perch close to the trunk in other kinds of trees, where they're easier to spot once autumn leaves fall. Some species roost inside tree cavities, and you may be able to spot them looking out of the holes on warm days.

Listen for an eastern screech-owl's whinnying or trilling at night.

Listen for Hints

Even though it's unlikely you'll hear one of these birds of prey flapping its wings because of the silencing flight feathers, your ears are still some of your best tools for discovery. Owls can be quite vocal, and like other bird groups, different species have different calls. Whether it's the *who-cooks-for-you* of the barred owl, the ghostlike trilling of a screech-owl or the bold, classic hooting of a great horned owl, learning their calls is one of the best things you can do to find more species right in your neighborhood.

Boost your owl know-how with the Cornell Lab of Ornithology's website, *allaboutbirds.org,* which includes calls for each bird species and is a great educational resource for all types of identification.

Hunt for Evidence

Beyond sight and sound, there are plenty of other ways to notice when an owl might be nearby. Like all birds, they molt their feathers and grow a new set every year. Be on the lookout for large feathers on the ground, and have a field guide handy to match your find with the correct species.

Owls produce pellets—little balls of indigestible hair and bone that they regurgitate. These remainders are sure signs that owls are around. Scour the ground beneath trees for owl pellets, and if you're feeling adventurous, take one apart to learn what the owls in your neighborhood have been eating for dinner.

ATTRACT MORE OWLS

Native plants are the best bet for attracting owls. Trees provide nesting places and shelter, and herbaceous plants offer habitat for prey. Go a step further and install boxes for cavity-nesting species, like screech-owls and barred owls.

The Ultimate Guide to Backyard Bird Photography

Get tips from a pro on how to turn your space into an ideal spot for capturing gorgeous scenes.

THE SCENE WAS PICTURE PERFECT. An adorable yellow-rumped warbler flitted down from the birch and landed on a bare branch. The bird, a male in spring plumage, paused for just a moment. My camera, focused on that very spot, needed no adjustment. I clicked the shutter. This perfect setup was no accident. I'd placed that dead branch right where I wanted it between the forest edge and my bird feeders.

Backyard bird photography can be amazing and rewarding. In fact, some of the best images of birds I've made have been from my very own porch. But to be successful, yard photography requires a bit of prep, planning and patience. Here are a few tips to get you started.

Habitat

To photograph birds, you have to provide a reason for them to visit. Natural landscaping using plants native to your region is the best tool to lure birds to your yard. Whether you live on a suburban lot or a sprawling rural spread, the species of plants that grow around your home will dictate the abundance and diversity of birds that visit.

I live on 10 hillside acres north of Fairbanks, Alaska. The birdlife here is highly seasonal, but during the brief spring and summer, quite a few species stop to visit. The lower portion of my property includes a small creek and some wetlands. This year a pair of solitary sandpipers raised a clutch of young by the creek, giving me a rare photo opportunity.

The forest begins just up the hill and is dominated by wild vegetation. The trees, a mix of birch, aspen and spruce, host the resident birds of the boreal forest: black-capped and boreal chickadees, redpolls, crossbills and gray jays. Seasonally, many migrants stop in to breed or rest during the summer.

Around the house is a small open yard where I've put my feeders. The food lures the birds from the trees out into the open, where it's easier to photograph them.

It's not very difficult to incorporate some of these basic elements into your own space, in different forms. A water feature, regardless of size, will bring in species that might not otherwise drop by. Insect-eating and aquatic birds won't usually visit a feeder, but if you provide some water you give them a good reason to stop. A small pond, even a few square feet, is often enough.

Native trees and shrubs are vital. These provide cover, food and a familiar habitat for local birds.

Tufted titmouse

Gray-headed junco

Food Sources

Carefully distributed food sources are crucial to improving your backyard bird photography. Several different types of feeders will get birds accustomed to visiting your yard. Before you start taking pictures, however, take down all but one feeder. This keeps the birds from flitting through in unpredictable ways. And having a single food source will help to focus their—and your—attention, for better photo opportunities.

Places to Perch

Feeders don't make photogenic perches. Plastic parts, wooden dowels and shelf feeders scattered with seed can look artificial and distracting. Instead, place natural-looking branches near your feeder. As birds visit, they'll land on these natural perches while they wait their turn at the seed or to investigate the food. Use only one or two branches, maximizing the chance that the birds will land where you want them. These perches should be close to where you will be shooting your images, particularly if you don't have a long telephoto lens. A position right outside your window can be a perfect location.

Backgrounds

Pay attention to what's behind your setup. Vegetation several yards back is best. If positioned well behind the bird, leaves will soften into pleasing washes of color. Colorful garden flowers can be a pretty addition, but be careful that they supplement your primary focus instead of distracting from it. Avoid houses, fences and vehicles; even blurred by distance, their geometric patterns cause distraction.

Light

Typically, morning and evening light are the best for photography. The low-angle sunlight at these hours provides a warm tone that flatters almost every subject. The drawback is that sunlight, no matter how warm, is directional. If it's bright, have the sun behind you so the bird doesn't have shadows crisscrossing its body. The diffuse light of a cloudy day is much easier to deal with. Direction doesn't matter as much, allowing you to concentrate on the compositions and backgrounds.

Equipment

I've purposely made it this far with no mention of a camera, because good photography has much less to do with your gear than with your creativity, dedication and planning. Your digital camera doesn't have to cost thousands of dollars and have a lens as long as your leg. Many of the point-and-shoots, and even cellphones, will take fine pictures if you've planned your setup. That said, a camera with good optics and decent

Townsend's warbler

Acorn woodpecker

Red-breasted nuthatch

resolution will of course help your images look their best. A tripod, even a cheap one from a discount store, provides a stable platform to shoot from.

Putting It All Together

Your perches are set up, the feeders are full, and the morning sun is peeking over your shoulder to bathe the scene in sweet light. Now the most important part of photography comes into play: patience. Wait. Remain as still as possible, pay attention and keep your finger on the shutter. The light will shift. Birds will come and go, somehow avoiding your perfect setup. You may get frustrated and think something needs to be adjusted, but resist the urge to move. Then, eventually, your quarry will appear. A bright songbird will land on the sunlit perch. Through the viewfinder, it will look startlingly handsome against the clean background. You smile. Click.

—*David Shaw*

DAVID'S QUICK TIPS FOR BETTER PHOTOS

REMEMBER COMPOSITION. Don't put your subject smack in the middle of the photo. If the bird is facing left, keep it on the right side of the frame. Don't get too close. Give the subject some breathing room in the photo for context.

TELL A STORY. A portrait of a perched bird against a clean background is good, but a picture that tells a story is much better. Photos of birds in flight, eating, singing or in courtship are more compelling.

KNOW YOUR CAMERA. Whether you are using a smartphone, a point-and-shoot or a professional-grade digital SLR, you've got to know how to use it. Read the manual and learn how to adjust settings quickly and without fuss.

PRACTICE. PRACTICE. PRACTICE. There are no secret shortcuts to becoming a good photographer. You've got to be out there taking photos, and lots of them.

DIOPTER RING
Move the ring to adjust this side's ocular lens. It allows for differences in your eyes and focuses your view correctly.

EYECUP
Here's a tip! If you wear glasses, the eyecups should be twisted down. Sans spectacles? Twist up.

OCULAR LENS
These lenses, closest to your eyes, magnify the object.

HINGE
It connects the two barrels. Hold the eyecups to your eyes and pivot the barrels until you see one circle-shaped image.

FOCUS WHEEL
Spin the wheel to move the ocular lenses simultaneously and bring the object into better focus.

OBJECTIVE LENS
These large lenses gather light. The bigger the lens, the more light it captures, which means a brighter scene.

BARRELS
The magic happens here! Each barrel works like a mini telescope to deliver a clear, crisp image.

Take a *Closer Look*

Discover how binoculars quickly bring your favorite birds into focus.

BEFORE YOU BUY
Go to a store and test out different brands and types of binoculars. Try them on to make sure they're not heavy on your neck or too bulky for your hands.

Many birdwatchers prefer an 8x42 model, a popular all-around size. That means an object appears eight times closer, and the objective lens diameter is 42 millimeters. The more

you pay, the better and more durable the "bins" will be, but you don't have to break the bank. Start with a waterproof model and work up from there per your preference.

What's your best advice for new birders?

Birds & Blooms readers share some words of wisdom for beginners.

OBSERVE BIRD BEHAVIORS and remember that there is always something new to learn. Get involved with citizen science projects like Project FeederWatch. Also, share your interest with others, especially young people.
Karen Holmes COOPER, MAINE

START WITH an open platform feeder full of black oil sunflower seed.
Nathan Lembke BENTONVILLE, ARKANSAS

INVEST IN A NICE FIELD GUIDE. Use it to check geographic locations to be sure the bird you're seeing should be in your area. Record the date you spotted it beside its name in your book.
Linda Gaff HUNTERTOWN, INDIANA

BUY THE BEST BINOCULARS your budget will allow. You'll have them for years, so make sure they're not too heavy and you feel comfortable carrying them.
Jannetta Tibbs ALBANY, OREGON

GET CONNECTED! Find your local Audubon Society chapter. They are always willing to help new birders.
Grace Huffman OKLAHOMA CITY, OKLAHOMA

YOU'LL HEAR more than you'll see. Learn bird calls ASAP. It'll be more enjoyable.
Patrick Hogan TEMPERANCE, MICHIGAN

A house wren sings a fast and musical series.

CHAPTER 2

Create a *Bird-Friendly* Habitat

Build a cozy and safe backyard with expert advice to keep your favorite fliers coming back year after year.

Make Your Backyard *Bird-Friendly*

A few clever gardening tricks to easily turn your landscape into a bird haven.

TRY YOUR HAND AT BIRDSCAPING, and you'll quickly learn that landscaping is for the birds—literally! Planting with birds in mind pays off fast, bringing more birds, more kinds of birds and longer visits from your friends. It's easy, too. All it takes is looking at your yard from a bird's point of view.

Birdscaping Basics

You'll have greater success at attracting your favorites when you realize two things—finding food and not getting eaten are the two biggest issues for birds.

Sure, you can just put out a tempting spread at the feeders, and birds will come. But to get them to linger, and maybe grace your place with a nest come spring, you'll need to make them feel safe, both while they're eating and while they're moving about the yard. This is the backbone of birdscaping.

"The more plants, the better," is a good motto. A yard that's chock-full of different trees, shrubs, grasses and vines, plus the usual flower beds, is what brings in the birds. One that's mostly lawn won't get many customers.

You might think food is the best way to get birds to your yard—and it is. Food is exactly what they're after on all those plants, including insects in incredible numbers and any tempting berries or fruit. But surprisingly, seed probably comes last when it comes to attracting birds.

TO ATTRACT a variety
of birds, try a grab-bag
approach. Planting a mix
of trees and shrubs in
your landscape will
broaden its appeal to
dozens of species and
extend its temptations
through the seasons.

Mulberries are tempting to rose-breasted grosbeaks.

Observe and Learn

You can learn a lot about planning for birds just by watching them in their natural surroundings. Observe them in your yard, and you'll see that very few of them spend time out in the open. Most birds move from one clump of plants to another. They alight in trees, gather in bushes or scoot through the garden looking for food. The sheltering branches or stems protect them from the hungry eyes of hawks, prowling cats and any of the other critters that are only too happy to dine on a dove, sparrow or chickadee.

So think like a wary bird and set up stepping-stones of shrubs, trees, grasses and flower beds. Go horizontal with corridors of plants so birds can move easily about your yard. A hedge of mixed berry bushes is irresistible to bluebirds, thrashers, catbirds and other friends. Groups of shrubs with just a hop, skip and jump between them are also great.

But think vertically, too, because birds move up and down as well as sideways. You can shoehorn in a surprising amount of cover by layering small trees, shrubs, ferns and ground covers near big trees, and by adding an arbor or trellises for vines and roses.

Thinking like a bird instantly reveals the benefit of including ornamental grasses, roses and other shrubs, as well as small trees, to your flower beds. Your backyard will soon look like an oasis, especially from the air.

8 WAYS TO PINCH THOSE PENNIES

- Dig suckers from lilacs, forsythia, serviceberry, weigela, shrub roses and other multiple-stemmed plants and transplant them to new homes.

- Trees and shrubs cost less at garden centers than nurseries. Selection is limited, and plants may not be as nicely shaped or as big, but the savings may get you three or four plants instead of just one.

- *Craigslist.com* often has free or cheap plants. Early birds get the worm.

- Scour the bulletin boards at supermarkets and other such places, and post your own notice for "Free Plants Wanted."

- Bare-root shrubs are a bargain. Look for bramble fruits, forsythia, hedge plants, and roses in bags rather than pots.

- Shop end-of-season sales to save a bundle.

- Scout the "sad sack" section of your nursery and garden center for damaged but possibly salvageable plants at cut-rate prices.

- Treasure every bird-planted tree seedling you find in your yard; transplant while still small.

Cardinals are attracted to flowering trees, like this weeping cherry, because of the insects that visit the blossoms.

Go Casual

While most gardeners strive for neatness, birds like messy surroundings, so birdscaping focuses on finding a happy medium—a natural look that will coax birds into lingering and possibly even nesting. Let perennials, shrubs and other plants knit together, instead of keeping bare space around every plant. Allow the dead leaves to lie beneath shrubs and hedges as an insect-rich mulch for gray catbirds, thrashers, wrens and other friends to investigate.

Hold off on cutting back flower beds until spring so goldfinches, titmice, doves, quail and other birds can shelter in them when searching for seeds and insects in winter. Instead of getting out the clippers every few months, learn to love the natural look of a free-form hedge.

Birds will appreciate it. And you'll appreciate the birds bringing life to your yard, every season of the year.

Junipers provide safe nesting sites for birds like this yellow-billed cuckoo.

Common
yellowthroat
on spiderwort

Cultivate the Ultimate *Habitat*

Establish a better, more sustainable space for your favorite
backyard birds, bugs, butterflies and wildlife with these ideas.

IF YOU LOVE BIRDS, there's a good chance you're already
planting, growing and gardening with them in mind. But
there's always a way to do more.

So what's the best way to maximize your backyard space
for local wildlife? And how do you get more bang for your
buck? Read on for the answers to these questions and more.

Now, keep in mind that it can take years for your yard
to reach its full potential, so don't let this list overwhelm
you. But that doesn't mean you can't make a difference now.
For starters, pick three things on this list to implement this
year—or more, if you're feeling ambitious. The birds, bugs,
butterflies and other wildlife in your area will thank you.

Make a Difference Through Gardening

START A NEW GARDEN SPACE JUST FOR WILDLIFE. If you don't already have a designated bird or butterfly garden, now is the time to create one. You'll find entire books and websites dedicated to the subject, so look around, consult some resources and start working on a space today.

EXPAND YOUR CANVAS WITH CONTAINERS. Don't have the space to start a whole new garden? No problem! Containers are a solution with style. Hanging baskets add flair and offer a good source of nectar. You'll be amazed by some of the new containers on the market, especially the self-watering ones.

GET RID OF INVASIVE PLANTS. Start by going online to *plants.usda .gov* and clicking on "Introduced, Invasive and Noxious Plants" on the left-hand side. You can search by state to see some of the invasive plants in your area. Once you know what they are, work to get them out as soon as possible.

PLANT MORE NATIVES. While you're ridding your yard of invasive plants, replace them with natives, which almost always suit the needs of local wildlife. Planting natives suited to your growing conditions will feed and shelter butterflies, birds and other creatures.

LOSE SOME GRASS. Most American backyards sport more grass than anything else. It might sound overwhelming to think about shrinking your lawn by half, so don't! Take it in stages instead. Put in a garden bed here and there. Before you know it, you'll have a slew of new wildlife-attracting plants and a lot less grass to mow.

DISCOVER A NEW KIND OF GRASS. Try designating an area for ornamental grass. Beauties such as prairie dropseed and Karl Foerster feather reed grass will feed birds and offer four-season appeal. Group them together, and you'll start to have a whole new appreciation for grasses.

NEVER UNDERESTIMATE THE VALUE OF A GOOD TREE. If you plan it right, a good tree can offer multiple benefits to wildlife, including nectar in spring, nesting space in summer, and berries in fall and winter. Go ahead and invest in a new tree for your backyard. You won't be sorry.

Bring in the Wildlife

PUT OUT A BUFFET. In addition to offering plants for wildlife, it's also good to put out different kinds of food. Of course, the birds and wildlife in your area will do just fine without it, but if you want an up-close view, this is the way to get it. Start by putting out black-oil sunflower seed and a sugar-water feeder. Then add items such as suet, thistle seed, safflower and peanuts as you like.

CREATE BENEFITS IN EVERY CORNER by planting containers with bird and butterfly favorites. Include native grasses in your landscape and add a birdbath to maximize your efforts.

CHECK YOUR BIRDHOUSES.
Many commercial birdhouses are more decorative than useful, so be sure to do your homework. For instance, if you want to attract bluebirds, make sure you have a bluebird house with the right dimensions, and hang it in the right area. Do a little research to learn about dimensions for different species before you buy. (See page 252 for birdhouse guidelines for common backyard birds.)

DON'T FORGET ABOUT THE BUTTERFLIES. Nectar-rich plants bring in butterflies, so you have lots of options there. But don't forget host plants for their eggs and caterpillars, such as milkweed for monarchs. Look for butterfly gardening resources in your area.

OFFER SOME WATER. Along with food and shelter, water is one of the three necessities of every backyard habitat. A larger water feature is desirable, but at the least, consider adding a birdbath. Birds will flock to it, especially in the heat of summer.

REDUCE PESTICIDE USE.
When you have caterpillars, bugs, butterflies and young birds exploring your backyard in summer, the last thing you want is for them to be harmed by pesticides. Make an effort to reduce pesticide use for the health of wildlife.

KEEP CATS INSIDE. Yes, it's a hard one for you cat lovers, but even birding expert George Harrison, a cat owner himself, agrees with this one. Cats are a leading cause of songbird deaths, so it's best if they stay inside.

Think of the Big Picture

SET GOALS. Don't overdo it. Maybe your goal is to add three new native plants this year. Or maybe you have a more ambitious plan to start a whole new butterfly garden. Whatever it is, no matter how big or small, it's important to set goals each season and then follow through.

TURN YOUR YARD INTO AN EXPERIMENT. Citizen science projects such as eBird, Great Backyard Bird Count, NestWatch and more are looking for birders and gardeners like you to provide valuable data for researchers. Sign up to help benefit science for generations to come.

GET THE WHOLE FAMILY INVOLVED. Making your yard more wildlife-friendly will be a lot more fun if you can involve everyone in your family. Have a discussion early on about why you're doing this and what it means. Then note things to watch for and assign individual jobs.

SHARE YOUR SUCCESS WITH THE NEIGHBORS. Rethinking your backyard is an excellent first step, but involving others is when it really starts to make a difference. Let them know why you're reducing your lawn or putting up more bird feeders. If you can get a whole neighborhood involved, you'll see results much faster!

COMMIT TO CONSERVATION.
Audubon At Home is a program of the National Audubon Society that supports the establishment of better wildlife habitats. Go online to *athome.audubon.org* to learn more.

CERTIFY YOUR BACKYARD.
The National Wildlife Federation has one of the best-known programs with its Certified Wildlife Habitat, which lets you pledge to provide food, water and shelter in your yard. If you haven't yet certified your backyard (you probably already meet the requirements), now is the time. Go to *nwf.org* for more info.

AUDUBON'S AT HOME PROGRAM OFFERS THESE SIMPLE "DO MORE, DO LESS" IDEAS:

MORE
Bird feeders
Native plants
Water features
Nest sites

LESS
Turf lawn
Free-roaming cats
Invasive plants
Impervious hardscaping

HUMMINGBIRD HABITAT

PLANT NATIVES THEY'LL LOVE. Bee balm, phlox and salvia are just a few of the native perennials that hummingbirds can't resist. To attract these jeweled fliers, remember that natives are always best.

DON'T FORGET TO OFFER LOTS OF RED. It's definitely true—hummingbirds love red. So be sure to plant enough scarlet flowers to keep them coming back for more.

CHOOSE A COMBO THAT BLOOMS FROM SPRING THROUGH FALL. You don't want all your flowers to fade just when fall migration is starting. Plan carefully so that you'll always have something to offer.

MIGRATION TIME IS KEY. Spring and late summer are big times for attracting hummingbirds. Even if you don't have regular summer visitors, don't give up just yet.

MAKE SURE YOUR SUGAR-WATER FEEDERS ARE FILLED. You don't want visitors to lose interest in your yard. Keep feeders full so the birds will stay around all summer. And be sure to change the sugar water regularly.

KEEP THE WATER COMING. Hummingbirds especially love mists.

Ruby-throated hummingbird at foxglove

Backyard Birding in Small Spaces

Even if you have just 100 square feet and not a 100-acre landscape, you can still attract birds. With small spaces, though, you'll need to maximize the opportunities. This can take planning, but the key points remain the same. Birds need the habitat basics of food, water and shelter. If you provide these three essentials, the visitors will come—no matter where you live or how tiny your space.

GARDEN FOR BIRDS

Planting a garden, even in containers, provides shelter and natural food for birds. Goldfinches (far left) are among the birds you can attract with plants.

Eastern towhees are ground feeders, but they will occasionally visit platform feeders for seed.

Maximize Space with a Variety of Food and Feeders

Be patient when you first put out a feeder. It can take the birds quite a while before they feel comfortable around a new one. After the first birds start using it, others will be quick to take notice.

There are endless varieties of birdseed on the market, but start with the basics when you have limited space. Thistle is an especially popular seed for American goldfinches, pine siskins and redpolls, with the bonus of being less attractive to squirrels. A thistle (Nyjer) tube feeder is a great choice for a small backyard.

Black oil sunflower seed is the pizza of bird food: Nearly everyone in the backyard will enjoy it. You can offer other quality seeds like safflower or even peanuts to satisfy other birds.

Another way to enhance your backyard is to offer different styles of bird feeders. While many species will readily perch at tube feeders, others prefer a larger platform to sit on. You can hang feeders almost anywhere; try a hook that hangs from the branch of a tree. Mount feeders along a porch railing. You can also plant an arch in the ground and make your own feeding station. Resist the urge to place a feeder in the center of your backyard, where the birds will have no shelter. Instead, put up several feeders in opposite corners of the yard. Or try moving a feeder closer to your house for better viewing.

Common redpolls don't mind sharing one feeder.

Thistle feeders attract a large variety of birds like these pine siskins.

Even One Birdbath Will Do Wonders

Water can be even more effective than food in luring birds close. From the simple to the most decorative, there are countless birdbath styles available. Or you can craft your own out of almost anything.

Be sure to change the water every day. It can get dirty surprisingly quickly. Also, stagnant water can be a breeding pool for mosquitoes and other insects. You should give the birdbath a good scrubbing on occasion as well.

Fountains, spinners or misters are a nice touch; the movement can help attract more birds. It's worth adding a couple of rocks to your birdbath, too. Beyond keeping the bath securely in place, they'll give the birds a better perch to drink or bathe from. Remember that most birds don't want water that is too deep. A couple of inches is plenty.

In winter you can add a birdbath heater. Some of these perform better than others, so check for reviews. Some of the most effective heaters are built right into the birdbath. There are also separate heaters that sit in most any tray. Remember that glass birdbaths should be brought in for the winter.

NO BACKYARD? NO PROBLEM!

Even if you live in a small apartment building or simply don't have a yard, you can still enjoy the birds. You'll be relying on surrounding habitats, but with careful observation, you can spot birds. Here's how:

WINDOW FEEDERS. There are feeders you can put right on your windows with suction cups. Use a suction cup suet feeder to get close-up looks at chickadees, nuthatches and woodpeckers.

HANGING BASKETS. Try displaying some hummingbird-friendly flowers. In addition to hummers, you could also attract beautiful butterflies and maybe even a sphinx moth.

INVEST IN OPTICS. You may see migrating birds in the treetops from an apartment window. Also, watch for flocks of ducks, geese, gulls and even swans flying along shorelines like Lake Michigan.

LOOK TO THE SKY. High-rise residents should look up for flying birds and not down toward the feeders. Peregrine falcons and red-tailed hawks patrol the skies in many urban areas, so keep your eyes to the sky.

FOCUS ON MIGRATION. It's exciting to host new visitors. Spring and fall migration offer the best chances of something unexpected showing up in your area. Stay alert!

KEEP IT COOL

Birds get hot, too! In the heat of summer, place your birdbath in the shade, if possible, and change the water out frequently.

Small Plants Do Double Duty

It's easy to overlook the importance of shelter to backyard birds. Sure, we all know birds need places to nest, but having some backyard plant cover can attract even more birds to your space all year.

Giving birds an easy place to retreat helps protect them from predators. Some people retire the holiday tree to the backyard so it can provide shelter year round. Sprinkling some cracked corn or sunflower seed near the shelter might help entice species like thrashers, towhees and juncos. These birds rarely come to more traditional feeders, but they feel right at home feeding on the ground near cover.

Consider planting native berries. With a berry-producing tree or shrub, you'll offer both protection and a bonus food source. Many shrubs provide good cover for birds.

Even a container shrub will help. Don't be surprised if a wren finds it a suitable place to build a nest. You can also put up a platform for robins or phoebes to use.

Especially with small backyards, it's important to remember that your space is just a part of the bird's home range. But with a little imagination, you can make even the tiniest of yards an ideal habitat.

Birds like American robins need only about 2 inches of water in birdbaths.

IT'S A MYTH that birds' feet will freeze to their next perch after they go for a dip in a heated birdbath. Water runs right off their scaly feet and waterproof feathers.

Water for *Wildlife*

Discover why birdbaths are essential in the winter.

FOOD IS AN EASY WAY to attract wildlife to your backyard, but there's something even more appealing. Water is the real magnet!

Wild animals typically view your garden as just one of many food hot spots within their range. Water sources, on the other hand, can be much farther apart and harder to find or get to. So if you have one in your yard, it's almost guaranteed to result in many feathered and furred visitors. Best of all, this is true whether we're in the depths of winter or in the heat of summer.

Understanding the Need

Offering water during the sweltering heat is intuitive. When it's hot out, it's easy to remember to keep your birdbath or water garden filled as you go about your gardening chores. During the winter, however, we tend to stay indoors and aren't thinking about offering water. But the animals are still there and still thirsty.

Many migratory birds use your region as winter habitat, migrating south from their summer breeding grounds. There's no shortage of year-round residents, either, including chickadees, nuthatches, finches, woodpeckers, bluebirds, mockingbirds, sparrows, cardinals, jays, wild turkeys and even some raptors. In addition, some mammals hibernate in winter, but many stay active throughout the year. This adds up to a lot of potential visitors looking for something to drink.

It's true that providing water can be more difficult when it's cold out, partly because we're not outside as much and we don't think about it, but also because simply topping off your birdbath or fountain every week or so just won't cut it when temperatures drop below freezing.

This makes providing water in winter all the more critical. When water freezes but no snow is on the ground, there is no way for wildlife to get moisture. At these times, the water you offer can mean life instead of death.

Options in the Backyard

The easiest way to provide water is by keeping a birdbath. If your winter temperatures dip below freezing, you can use a birdbath heater, an inexpensive electric device that keeps the water just above the freezing point. There are also solar-powered models. But it can be just as simple to dump the ice out each morning and refill the bath—as long as you remember to do it.

If you want to offer a larger water feature, like a pond, the size will determine when the water will freeze and become unavailable for drinking. The bigger the surface area and greater the depth, the less likely it will be to freeze completely. So if you're installing such a feature, make it as big as your space and budget allow.

Similarly, moving water takes longer to freeze than still water, so think about a pump and a waterfall. It will sound nice at any time of year, and it could be the only place wildlife can grab a drink for weeks or even months.

However you choose to provide water in winter, know that you'll be helping birds and other creatures to survive this harsh season. And you'll be helping yourself to guaranteed wildlife-watching opportunities right outside your window.

WHAT ABOUT SNOW?

During icy winters when all available water is frozen solid, birds and other wildlife will eat snow as a source of life sustaining moisture. This costs them extra energy, because some of their body heat goes into melting the snow. As long as they're eating well, this isn't a problem.

NEAT AND TIDY

Clean water keeps hummingbirds coming back. Reader Lisa Swanson of Maricopa, Arizona, whose photos are featured here, has this advice: "I disassemble my fountain and use a brush and warm water to clean it every two to three days, then refill it with fresh water."

Backyard *Showers*

Attract more hummingbirds to your space with moving water.

MOST BACKYARD BIRDS love to bathe and splash around in a clean birdbath, hummingbirds included! Although they occasionally stop at a shallow bath for a dip, these tiny birds prefer to wet their feathers by flying through or sitting under a gentle spray. One of the best ways to transform your landscape into a hummingbird hub is to incorporate a moving water feature.

Unlike other birds, hummingbirds want a light shower instead of a complete soak because their primary concern is simply to get their feathers clean. Most of their other hydration needs are met by all the sugar water and liquid flower nectar they slurp up.

Hummingbirds rinse off in the rain, at splashing streams or in the spray of waterfalls, and you can re-create the same kind of natural showers they love in your own backyard. It's easy!

To set up an inexpensive solar fountain, you'll need a basin deep enough to submerge a small pump or hold a floating model. The basin should be wide enough to catch and recycle the falling spray. A classic pedestal birdbath can work; its basin is usually both wide and deep. But because it may be too deep for hummingbirds, you should add stones if needed to keep the water shallow.

Maintenance is fairly simple, too. Make sure to keep an eye on the water level, especially on windy days. Refill the basin as needed to assure that the pump doesn't run dry.

The best thing about a solar fountain is that you don't need an electrical outlet, so you can put the birdbath almost anywhere. Just be sure that the small solar panel, attached by a cord to the pump, is in direct sunlight. The fountain will temporarily stop spraying on overcast days or if a large cloud moves across the sun.

An Anna's hummingbird splashes in a backyard bubbler.

Once you have a solar fountain bubbling away, it's time to amp things up. Add a tiny perch beside it so you can watch one of these busy birds for a few extra minutes as it stops to buzz its wings and contort its body to catch every drop of water.

To make a good resting spot, choose a slim branching stick (about 4 feet long) with twigs skinny enough for tiny feet to easily grasp. Dead, twiggy branches that fall from maples and other deciduous trees make ideal perches. Push the bottom of the stick into the soil beside the basin to anchor it. It's even better if part of the branch extends through the spray, so hummingbirds can have a spot right in the droplets.

Then just sit back and enjoy some special moments of watching those zipping, preening hummingbirds in your backyard showers.

Say Hello to Hummingbirds

Follow the chart for quick solutions to attract and feed hummingbirds.

Want to attract more hummingbirds?

Do you have?

A LARGE GARDEN

LUCKY!
You can go crazy with plants and bushes hummingbirds love—cannas, fuchsia, pentas, hibiscus, salvia and columbine, to name just a few. Plant them all together for a real hummingbird haven.

A SMALL SPACE

DON'T WORRY.
Hummingbirds visit patios and balconies, too, with the right mix of plants. Try phlox, verbena, calibrachoa and petunias, which are all easy-care container plants.

ONE FEEDER

NO PROBLEM.
Since it's the only feeder you've got, make it count. Keep a close eye on it to make sure it's never empty, or the hummingbirds will lose interest. For a little extra impact, hang a basket of red impatiens nearby.

SEVERAL FEEDERS

KEEP 'EM HAPPY.
To encourage several hummingbirds to visit regularly, space feeders out of sight of each other to prevent territorial competition. Try providing perches or even a misting water feature. Watching them fly through the mist is cheery entertainment, too.

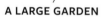

I've got hummingbirds, but I need some solutions to these feeder problems.

ANTS OR BEES HAVE TAKEN OVER MY FEEDER.

LET'S GET THIS FIXED.
For bees, make sure your feeder is equipped with bee guards. The best defense against ants is an ant moat, which is essentially just a cup of water hanging above your feeder to keep the ants from reaching the feeding port.

THE SUGAR WATER GOES BAD SO QUICKLY.

DON'T LET IT SPOIL.
If possible, hang your feeder in the shade. And remember, it's crucial to keep the feeder clean and the sugar water fresh. (Don't forget, the recipe is 4 parts water to 1 part sugar.) If the sugar water is cloudy, it's time to replace it.

MY FEEDER IS SO HARD TO CLEAN.

YOU'RE NOT ALONE!
Some readers swear that an old toothbrush or bottle brush will reach all the crevices of a hummingbird feeder. Or try mixing a tablespoon of uncooked rice and water in the feeder and shaking vigorously. Rinse the feeders well after any cleaning.

Birdbath *Basics*

For a robust bird population, just add fresh water!
Lure more species to your backyard with these six tips.

1. Shallow basins are best. The water should be no deeper than 2 inches in the middle and ½ to 1 inch at the edges.

2. Place rocks or stones in the middle of your bath for birds to perch and drink without getting their feet wet.

3. Nestle baths in a shady spot (to keep the water fresh) that is near trees or shrubs, but not so near that predators can lurk in ambush. When a bird is taking a dip and a predator flies by, it needs a safe place to go.

WATER IS THE TICKET to attracting a variety of species, even those that shy away from feeders.

4. Add motion with a dripper, fountain or mister. The noise and movement catches a bird's attention better than standing water. Bonus: Hummingbirds love a light mist!

5. Clean and rinse your bath every couple of days and then add fresh water. Grab a wire brush for a deep clean if algae forms.

6. Pedestal baths allow you to watch birds splish-splashing around right from your window. Consider a ground-level bath, too. It mimics natural water sources and lures birds that like to stay low.

BIRDBATH IN A SNAP!
Your feathered friends won't mind if you recycle. Give a trash can lid, old pan or flowerpot tray new life as a quick and easy birdbath.

Purchase birdbaths at your local big-box store, garden center, specialty bird store or online.

BACK OFF

When birds start using a nest box, give them their space. It's best to observe and photograph the miracle of life from a distance.

Birdhouse *FAQs*

Make your yard more appealing to nesting birds with these easy tips and solutions.

Do birds use birdhouses all summer?

The short answer is yes. While springtime might be best known for being nesting season, several bird species will raise two, three or even four or more broods in a single season. So keep those houses up—you can attract nesters all summer.

When should I plan to take birdhouses down?

Just because nesting season is over doesn't mean you have to put your birdhouses away. Instead, leave them up because they make great roosting boxes. You should still clean out your birdhouses, though. Fall is the best time to do so.

Do birdhouses have specific size requirements?

Yes! The type of bird you attract with a nest box has a lot to do with the dimensions of it, both the overall size and the hole openings. For a list of birdhouse guidelines for common backyard species, go to page 252. This handy chart also gives hanging height.

Should birdhouses and feeders be placed together?

No. It's best to keep birdhouses away from feeders. Parent birds are territorial when it comes to their nest, and it could jeopardize the young by putting feeders nearby where lots of birds will be coming and going.

How many different species use birdhouses?

Nearly 50 different bird species in North America will use a birdhouse. Some of the most popular birds you can attract include titmice, bluebirds, swallows, wrens, chickadees and woodpeckers. For larger birds, you can even attract screech-owls and wood ducks.

If a birdhouse isn't getting used, how can I increase the chances?

First, make sure that you have a birdhouse that fits the right guidelines. Many decorative houses will have an entrance hole that is too large. Or some birdhouses are really flashy and complicated, so birds don't feel comfortable using them. The more you can do to make a birdhouse look and feel natural, the better chance you'll have at it being used. You can also put a little bit of nesting material in the house, enticing birds to check it out.

If a birdhouse is taken over by house sparrows, what should I do?

You can trap sparrows because they aren't a protected North American bird. You can also remove their nesting material regularly to keep them from getting too cozy. Otherwise, take your houses down for a little while to encourage them to move on to another area.

Be an Owl *Landlord*

Roll out the welcome mat for these shadowy nighttime fliers.

Barn owls may raise their young inside man-made structures, like nest boxes, barns and even homes.

OWLS ARE BOTH POPULAR and mysterious. They're so obscure, in fact, that most people report they've never seen one in real life. But some kinds of owls come into suburban neighborhoods and city parks, and they might even call your backyard home when you follow these four tips.

1. Provide Shelter

Most kinds of owls like to hide inside dense cover during the day and venture out only at night. Evergreen trees provide this kind of shelter year-round. Depending on where you live, ideal choices include pine, spruce or juniper; check with a local native plant nursery to find out which grows best in your region. Eventually you may find long-eared owls, northern saw-whet owls, great horned owls or other species nestled away among the branches, sleeping the day away.

2. Offer Nest Sites

Eastern screech-owls are common and widespread east of the Rockies, with western screech-owls replacing them farther west, and both often lurk in towns and cities. However, to nest and raise young, they need cavities such as woodpecker holes or natural hollows in trees. If you can safely leave dead trees or large dead limbs standing, these often have holes that owls use. Otherwise, screech-owls use nest boxes designed for wood ducks or American kestrels, with an entrance hole at least 3 inches in diameter. In cooler climates, the northern saw-whet owl also adopts nest boxes, although it favors a 2-inch entrance hole.

Some larger owls also nest in cavities, including barn and barred owls. If you live in farm country, you may be able to place a barn owl box at the edge of open fields or in a barn loft. Barred owls favor dense, swampy woods, and they like boxes that are high in trees.

3. Say No to Insecticides

To successfully lure owls to your space, you have to also attract the creatures they hunt. Screech-owls feed on large insects, such as moths and beetles, and small animals such as mice. If you use insecticides or rodenticides around your garden, those poisons may wipe out the prey before the owls find them. Worse, the poisons may be passed along directly to the owls.

4. Keep Cats Indoors

Even if they're well-fed, prowling house cats kill many small wild animals. Wiping out populations of mice, voles, lizards and other creatures may not leave enough to support a family of screech-owls or other small owls. On the flip side, a cat that wanders outside at night might become a meal for a large species like a great horned owl. It's better for everyone to keep house cats inside houses where they belong!

To lure eastern screech-owls, hang a nest box in February.

A SPOT FOR OWLS

Buy nest boxes that are designed for screech-owls or larger owls, or build your own. Check out *theraptortrust.org* for building plans, advice on placement and more.

CHAPTER 3

Feeding 101

The way to a bird's heart is through its stomach! Learn how to feed them no matter the conditions.

Feed More Birds *Year-round*

Attract more birds to your backyard
this year with simple seasonal tips.

IT USED TO BE THAT MOST backyard bird-watchers
fed their visitors only in winter. Times have changed,
though, and birders realize how much fun it is to feed
birds year-round. To get more birds (and more kinds
of birds) at your feeder this year, just follow these
simple seasonal tips.

Winter

Not all birds head south in the winter. Lots of your
favorites, like cardinals, chickadees, nuthatches and
juncos, will stick with you through these cold, dark
months and maybe even brighten your days a bit.

Birds flock to feeders in winter, especially during
cold spells, heavy snows and ice storms. You'll want to
use large-capacity feeders so you don't have to trudge
through the snow as often to refill. Bring the feeders
up close to the house, since most of your viewing will
happen from inside.

Keep those seed feeders filled with a mix of mostly
sunflower and some white millet. Fill feeders in late
afternoon so food is available just before nightfall and
at daybreak, when birds need a boost after the long, cold
night. Add an extra suet feeder to give woodpeckers and
others another high-calorie dining spot.

Thistle is a winter must. Pine siskins, common
winter visitors, love this seed.

WINTER FRIENDS

Northern cardinals are some of the most popular winter visitors. Here, males and females share space at a feeder on a snowy day.

Spring

Springtime is when birds are most active. A wide variety of colorful songbirds are coming home to nest, while others are just passing through, so pull out all the stops by offering a banquet.

For seed, using a mix of black-oil sunflower, white millet and sunflower chips (sunflower seeds without the shells) will cover most of your spring bases.

Chickadees, nuthatches, house finches and cardinals love sunflower, and so do migrating rose-breasted grosbeaks. The millet that falls to the ground might attract migrating white-throated, white-crowned and chipping sparrows. Sometimes even buntings show up at a feeder this time of year if it has some white millet.

Warblers and robins might eat sunflower chips. Although these insect eaters can't crack shells easily, they'll eat chips. But by the time bugs become plentiful later in the spring, you probably won't see any warblers, buntings or tanagers at your seed feeders.

Suet is a favorite of woodpeckers all year, but in the spring, tanagers, warblers, bluebirds and kinglets also relish this high-energy treat. Feed live mealworms to bug-loving new arrivals like bluebirds, robins, wrens, warblers and mockingbirds. It's a nice high-protein snack.

Offering some nectar in the spring beckons hummingbirds and even orioles. Here's a spring must: Display fresh orange halves, meat side up, on a spike or dead tree branch. Orioles and tanagers can't resist them.

Summer

Summer means lots of hungry young bills to feed, with some birds having as many as four or five broods of babies. Even though nature provides plenty of bugs, berries and seeds, it's fun to watch fledglings flap their wings, squawk and beg their patient parents for food at your feeders.

Young and old birds alike will continue to eat your seed mix if it's loaded with black-oil sunflower. Chickadees, house finches, sparrows, cardinals, nuthatches and more will bring their babies to your seed feeders for a lesson in finding an easy lunch.

Suet eaters like woodpeckers are around all summer and love to bring the family over for a bite. Often, when you see several woodpeckers together at a suet feeder in the summer, you're

Baltimore oriole

Eastern bluebirds

CHANGE IT UP

Adjust your offerings throughout the year to attract the most species of birds. From mealworms and fresh oranges in spring and summer to nuts in the autumn, your feathered friends will love the variety.

Red-breasted
nuthatch

seeing parents teaching their big, awkward babies where to find a snack.

Both seed and suet eaters are attracted to seed cylinders if they're heavy on sunflower and nuts. These large cylinders can take a long time to empty and need little maintenance, making them perfect when you're away on vacation.

Goldfinches are sought-after visitors all year but are only bright yellow in the summer. Feed fresh thistle (Nyjer) all summer long to attract these beauties.

Summertime is hummer time, which means sugar water is a must. If you surround your feeder with honeysuckle, salvia or trumpet vine, you should see increased hummingbird action, especially in mid- to late summer as young ones join their parents at the feeder.

Autumn

Think of fall as spring migration in reverse, only with more birds, including young ones making their first trip south.

Feed a mix with sunflower, millet and chips to see some of the same migrants you saw last spring. Watch for white-crowned, white-throated and chipping sparrows as they move through.

Warblers and kinglets might join the year-round woodpeckers and nuthatches at your suet feeder. The arrival of the juncos every fall is the highlight of the season for many. Juncos stick around all winter and love to eat millet from the ground.

Orioles may make a pit stop at your jelly or nectar feeder as they head south. Hummingbird activity often peaks in September as local parents and babies join migrants from further north on the road to Mexico or Central America.

Year-round residents like cardinals, woodpeckers, nuthatches, jays and chickadees are hunkering down for the winter, and they are looking for regular sources of food and cover to get them through the cold months ahead.

Keep your seed and suet feeders filled so your yard becomes a regular stop on their feeding circuit. Make sure your seed feeder has enough space so larger birds like cardinals and grosbeaks are comfortable. A hopper feeder, tray feeder or tube feeder with a tray all work well.

You might consider adding a ground feeder this time of year, too. Also, freely toss seed mix loaded with millet on the ground in several places around your yard. Then lots of juncos, migrating sparrows and towhees can spread out to eat with plenty of elbow room.

Bird Feeding Seasonal Checklist

Hairy woodpecker

American goldfinches

WINTER

- Chickadees, nuthatches, brown creepers, jays and woodpeckers all love peanut pieces. Add some to your seed mix, or hang a special peanut feeder to attract extra attention.
- High-fat, high-calorie suet is the perfect food to help birds get through longer nights and colder temps. Don't be afraid to place them right outside your window for prime viewing.
- Put out a seed block, making sure it's heavy on high-fat sunflower and nuts that birds love. Avoid seed balls with mostly millet and milo.
- After the holidays, recycle your Christmas tree to give birds some convenient cover. You can also hang up seed ornaments and other treats.

SPRING

- Don't stop feeding the birds just because it's warming up. Less of their natural food is available in early spring than at any other time of the year, since most berries and seeds from plants have been eaten throughout the winter and little growth has begun. It's also too early for insects, so keep the food coming!
- Starlings, grackles and squirrels can dominate feeders, so consider switching to safflower to break their habit, since they don't like it. Also focus on thistle for a while, bringing in beauties like goldfinches.
- Fresh oranges will lure orioles to your backyard and might even tempt tanagers, grosbeaks and house finches. Apple halves attract cardinals, mockingbirds, woodpeckers and others.
- Many think of suet as a fall and winter treat, but it's also a secret weapon for attracting spring migrants like warblers, tanagers and kinglets.

Ruby-throated
hummingbird

Black-billed
magpie

SUMMER

- Make nectar for hummingbirds by mixing 4 parts water to 1 part white sugar. In hot weather, sugar water can ferment quickly, so change the nectar in your feeder at least twice a week. Don't give up if you don't attract them right away.

- Thistle seed (Nyjer) is definitely more expensive, but it's a real treat for finches. Buy it in bulk and store in a cool, dry place.

- Frequently replenish birdbath water during hot weather. Maintain a depth of no more than a couple of inches to allow birds to stand while bathing.

- Bluebirds and robins love bugs. Try feeding live or roasted mealworms to entice these insect eaters.

AUTUMN

- Don't take your sugar-water feeder down until late fall. No, it doesn't interfere with hummingbird migration, and you just might get some stragglers.

- Double the number of seed and suet feeders around your yard as birds are currently flocking, and there are more mouths to feed.

- Switch to hopper-style feeders, which are more practical than tray feeders at times when the moisture from rain and snow can ruin food. Tube feeders work well in inclement weather, too.

- Check the condition of your feeders and squirrel baffles to make sure they will make it through winter. Replace the ones you can't repair.

Gray catbird

10 Things You Aren't Feeding Birds...*Yet*

Don't limit your birds to seed, suet and sugar water. Make your buffet the best on the block to keep 'em coming back for more.

WHEN WAS THE LAST time you added a new feeder to your backyard? Or put out a special treat for the birds? Even if you've been feeding backyard birds for years, there are probably a few things you haven't tried yet. And adding new items is the best way to attract a wider variety of species to your space. Give one of these fun food options a try and see what you can attract.

Peanut Butter

I know many folks who've stopped buying suet cakes and now make their own, with peanut butter as the base. Others have made the switch from feeding peanuts, either in or out of the shell, to offering peanut butter instead. You can stuff the holes of a log feeder with peanut butter or just smear it on tree bark.

BIRDS THAT LIKE ORANGES

Gray catbirds	Brown thrashers
Red-bellied woodpeckers	Orioles
Northern mockingbirds	Tanagers

Baltimore oriole at jelly feeder

Woodpeckers and blue jays relish peanut butter snacks. You can also put it out for species like nuthatches that will store caches of peanuts but would be hard-pressed to stock up on jars of peanut butter!

Jelly

What goes better with peanut butter than jelly? Grape jelly is becoming a go-to offering for orioles. Gray catbirds and red-bellied woodpeckers are among the other species that can't resist the sweet, fruity stuff. You can buy a special jelly feeder, but any shallow container will also do the trick.

Fruit

Many lodges in the tropics offer fruit to draw birds in for close viewing. Tanagers are keen on these fruit feeding stations, and some folks who live farther north have been fortunate enough to lure the brilliantly colored western, summer and scarlet tanagers to their own backyards. Orioles love orange halves; when they've eaten the fruit, fill the empty peels with jelly. Also try putting out berries or raisins, or experiment with any fruit you happen to have. You just might attract mockingbirds or robins.

Butterflies flock to fruit, too. I've used a window feeder to offer apples and bananas and had great success attracting these pretty fliers.

Mealworms

Try adding mealworms to your buffet. Some people have success with oven-roasted worms, while others swear by the live ones. I keep a container of the latter in my refrigerator door, and the only real maintenance is to toss in a carrot for them once in a while (they need to eat, too!). Mealworm feeders need to be a couple of inches deep so the worms won't crawl out. Although it might take the birds a while to find your mealworms, once they do, they'll be hooked. Mealworms are like candy to them. I offer a dozen or so at a time. The birds will quickly train you to feed them on a regular schedule by scolding you when you slack off.

Mealworms appeal to a wide range of birds, including some species that don't usually come to traditional feeders. Some of the most common are bluebirds and robins.

FROM LEFT: CAROL L. EDWARDS; KATHY ADAMS CLARK/KAC PRODUCTIONS

Red-bellied woodpecker with mealworms

THE LEAST PICKY EATERS

No matter what you're serving, these birds will eat it.

BLUE JAYS. They'll eat just about anything and are not bashful about it.

RED-BELLIED WOODPECKERS. Known for munching on seed, suet, fruit, mealworms and many other offerings.

GRACKLES. They're not just less picky eaters, they're also some of the messiest.

ONE OF THE BEST ways to diversify your backyard feeding station is to garden for birds. Plant some native berries or fruit trees.

Cedar waxwing with serviceberries

Roasted Seeds

Plenty of birds are seed eaters, but you can think beyond the usual sunflower and safflower varieties. Try roasting pumpkin or squash seeds; you can bake up a batch, share half with the birds, plain, and season the other half to your own liking. Then you'll be snacking right along with the birds that you're watching. Northern cardinals, sparrows and other seed specialists will especially enjoy the variety.

Baked Eggshells

These provide calcium, which can be especially important for females during nesting season. But it's essential that you wash and bake the shells to kill off any potential pathogens. You wouldn't want to give your feathered guests food poisoning or something even worse. After you bake the shells, crush them and add them to your seed, or just sprinkle them on the ground. You can also offer them in a platform feeder.

Compost

When I was growing up, my grandpa had the biggest compost pile ever. I remember hauling out the scraps in an old ice cream bucket and tossing them on the pile. I also remember that black-billed magpies were always eager to greet me at the pile. Just remember that your compost pile is fair game for other critters, too. I could always count on spotting a raccoon at my grandpa's after dark.

Stale Nuts

It seems like there are always some leftover nuts around, especially during the holidays. If you've got unsalted nuts that are past their prime, put them out and see which birds will take a bite.

Plants

This one might sound obvious, but its importance can't be overstated. One of the best ways to diversify your backyard feeding station is to garden for birds. (And not just for hummingbirds.) Go ahead and plant some native berries or fruit trees, or let your flowers go to seed, and you'll reap the avian rewards in all seasons.

HERE'S A TIP—and it's an important one. Though it has been a tradition for decades, experts say you should not feed bread to birds because it can lead to nutritional problems.

Suet Creations

Traditional suet is made of beef fat, but *Birds & Blooms* hears frequently from readers who rave about their homemade suet recipes. Some use lard, peanut butter, coconut, raisins, birdseed and much more to make suet cakes. Experiment with those foods and see what tasty bird treats you can come up with!
—*Ken Keffer*

WHAT NOT TO FEED BIRDS

Chocolate	Bread
Table scraps	Other baked goods
Potato chips	

FROM LEFT: RICHARD DAY/DAYBREAK IMAGERY; JOHN GILL

NO. 1 FANS

Goldfinches, like this American goldfinch, are well-known thistle eaters, but these seeds also draw pine siskins, redpolls, and many other finches.

The Thing *About Thistle*

Learn where this popular seed comes from and why it's a bird favorite.

TUBE OR SOCK FEEDERS full of thistle seed are a common way to welcome songbirds into your garden. But the next time you refill your feeders, consider this: The seeds you're buying at the store aren't what you might think. They don't come from the plant we know as thistle here in North America. What's in the package is another seed that's just as tasty and healthy for backyard birds.

"When people refer to thistle seed that goes in feeders, they're generally not talking about the seed that comes from either native or invasive thistle. They're talking about Nyjer," said John Rowden, director of community conservation at the National Audubon Society.

Nyjer seeds come from the African yellow daisy, a plant not commonly grown in the United States. The seeds are collected and sold by communities in northern Africa. Before they're exported, the seeds are sterilized so the plant doesn't become invasive in other environments.

It sounds like a lot of work to prepare this simple seed, but John said Nyjer's value to birds makes the effort worthwhile. "It has a good combination of protein, fat and fiber, and that's great as a winter bird food when fliers are trying to gain that high caloric content," he said. Some companies market the same birdseed under the name "niger."

Nyjer is suited for attracting finches, chickadees, pine siskins, juncos, sparrows, mourning doves and buntings, among others. John recommends using mesh socks or specialized tube feeders to share the seed, as they are designed to provide ample places for small birds to cling on.

Field editor Kathy Eppers has one tried-and-true suggestion. "Hang the thistle feeder away from your other feeders. It seems the goldfinches and house finches are most apt to feed when they are in an area that's quiet, without the hustle and bustle of large birds like jays," she said. Placement in the open, but near cover, also helps birds keep an eye out for predators.

Serve thistle in any season, but always keep it fresh. Throw out the whole lot if seeds get too wet. As a benchmark, field editor Patrick Hogan said he analyzes the seeds' shininess to determine freshness. If they look dull, he puts out a fresh batch of seed.

Besides serving store-bought seeds, John recommends planting native thistle to naturally bring feathered friends to your backyard. Visit *audubon.org/plantsforbirds* to find out what options are native in your area.

PICKY EATERS

Nyjer seeds are tiny, but they still have a shell. If you think your backyard birds might be just pecking at their food—not eating it—check the ground litter for thin hulls.

Serve a *Fruity Feast*

Go beyond oranges and add more sweet treats to your backyard menu.

THE BEST WAY to get a new backyard fruit feeder noticed is to have a hungry bird already picking at its offerings.

Luckily for birders, orioles have that role covered. Once they arrive from their wintering grounds and locate a consistent buffet of halved oranges, the vivid birds become late-spring feeder regulars. Their presence may attract colorful tanagers and rose-breasted or black-headed grosbeaks, which return from the tropics about the same time as orioles.

"We offer fresh oranges when fruit-eaters such as orioles are most likely to visit—the spring and summer months," says Emma Greig, who keeps an eye on the bird feeders at the Cornell Laboratory of Ornithology at Sapsucker Woods. She also manages all aspects of Project FeederWatch, the lab's popular winter-long feeder survey with thousands of participants. Like any backyard bird lover, she is delighted when the orioles return from their winter grounds.

Oranges are a super easy and convenient mainstay, but the produce aisle offers more options. Try any fruit you have on hand, including bananas, mangoes or papayas. Tanagers, grosbeaks and other neotropical migrants respond especially well to these and other fruits found in their winter homelands.

In summer, the abundance of insects and natural fruit, as well as nesting duties, naturally causes feeder traffic to drop. But ripe peaches, pears, grapes or other sweet treats still attract resident house finches, downy woodpeckers, wrens, cardinals, robins and orioles. Other crucial pollinators also may be drawn to the sugary snacks—bees, wasps and butterflies.

You might think of fruit only as a warm weather treat, but the birds that love it most are found year-round in many regions. Offer dried fruit or apple halves (which are edible even when frozen) from late fall through winter to attract bluebirds, American robins, northern cardinals, gray catbirds, brown thrashers, hermit thrushes, northern mockingbirds, wrens, and downy and other woodpeckers.

Lately, robins are becoming more frequent year-round guests at backyard feeders. Emma says that reported sightings and photos sent to Project FeederWatch show a definite rise in their winter visits.

Some store-bought seed mixes include dried fruit, and they "help attract a wider variety of species than pure seed mixes," notes Emma. "Personally, I would rather not have fruit mixed in with my seed, so that I don't have to offer the expensive fruit bits all the time. Do what works for your budget and backyard!"

UTILIZE A TRAY FEEDER

To get started, serve a small portion of your fruit of choice on a tray feeder to attract birds' attention. The open feeder helps birds spot the treats more quickly. Just like other food sources, place it next to some cover. Having trees, bushes, tall grass or other shelter nearby helps birds feel safer when approaching a new feeder.

FEED MORE BIRDS
Baltimore orioles, like this male, love oranges. But try setting out grapes, pears, apples or peaches and see what other fruit lovers show up!

Blue jay

THE GOOD FAT

Have you heard nuts are a good fat for people? This is true for birds as well. Peanuts not only provide protein for birds, they're also a fine source of unsaturated fat.

Peanuts in the Backyard

You'll be impressed with the variety of birds attracted by these snacks at your feeder.

Bring in the Jays

Peanuts are like a secret weapon for people who love to feed birds. They can be an expensive item to offer on a regular basis, but they'll bring in a wide variety of new birds. For example, jays seem to sense whenever peanuts are put out within a 5-mile radius. You won't see them in your yard for months or years, but as soon as you offer peanuts in a shell, they can appear within days or even hours!

Battling Squirrels

Yes, it's true that squirrels love peanuts just as much as birds. First of all—good luck. They sure can be persistent! However, there are a few peanut feeders out there that are designed to be squirrel-proof. Most are for out-of-shell peanuts. Otherwise, find a good squirrel baffle to keep those furry critters away. Another option—buy a peanut feeder designed for squirrels! Many readers swear by the theory that if you give the squirrels their own place to eat, they'll leave the bird area alone.

Shell vs. No Shell

At the end of the day, it doesn't matter—they're going to get eaten. But it can be fun to watch birds with those large, in-shell peanuts, taking them off to crack or cache. Keep in mind that they do require different feeders. So make sure you align your feeder with your feed.

Word of Warning

First off, don't offer salted peanuts or give birds your leftovers from the ball game. Next, if it's damp or rainy in your area, clean out those feeders because like other seed, peanuts can get moldy. If you know it's going to be rainy, conserve by just putting out a few peanuts at a time.

EXPERT ADVICE

"If you like offering peanuts but find them a bit pricey, mix out-of-shell peanuts with black oil sunflower seeds. Both can be fed from the same feeder."
—*Kimberly Kaufman*

PEANUT LOVERS

Peanut eaters may not show up right away. Remind yourself that it's worth the wait. Just look at the wide variety of birds you can lure to your backyard when you offer peanuts:

Jays	Magpies
Woodpeckers	Sparrows
Chickadees	House finches
Titmice	Cardinals
Nuthatches	

Get Savvy About Suet

Mix things up and bring in a whole new flock of birds by serving this popular treat.

What Is Suet?

From a technical perspective, suet is specifically the raw fat around kidneys and loins, mostly in beef. Because it's high in fat, it gives birds lots of energy, which is especially helpful in cold weather.

What Are Suet Cakes?

Suet cakes are actually what most people refer to as suet. They are usually made up of a mixture that includes suet (or rendered beef fat) as an ingredient. Other ingredients mixed in suet might include peanut butter, peanuts, seed, cracked corn and birdseed.

Make It or Buy It?

Whether you make your own or buy it from a store is up to you. If you buy it, check the ingredients for quality items. Of course, suet should have suet (or rendered beef fat) listed as an ingredient. If you want to make your own, hit up your local butcher shop and ask to buy the suet. It should be fairly inexpensive, and you can be sure it's what you need for the birds.

What's the Best Way to Serve?

In the simplest form, you can just smear suet onto a branch or a hollowed log—no special feeder required. Another option is a cage feeder, which you can pick up for a few bucks. This definitely does the trick without spending a lot of money. Finally, if you want to maximize your real estate, look for a special suet feeder that will hold several blocks at once.

Which Birds Eat Suet?

You can attract a wide range of birds, including chickadees, nuthatches, wrens, thrushes, creepers, thrashers, jays, and nearly all woodpeckers, including flickers. Even if you haven't seen these birds at your suet in other seasons, try again in fall and winter. You'll likely attract new visitors.

MAKE YOUR OWN SUET

You can find a lot of suet recipes out there, but it's fun to make up your own, too. Great suet is all about the right consistency. Mix and match the items on the "yes" list below. A good base is 1 cup of suet and 1 cup of peanut butter. Melt over low heat, and mix in ½ cup of cornmeal and ¼ cup of oats. Next, add ¼ cup of items like birdseed, nuts or berries until you get the right consistency. Freeze in muffin tins or in small plastic containers until you're ready to dole it out.

YES	NO
Raw suet	Bread
Black oil sunflower seeds	Sugar
Unsalted nuts	Leftovers
Dried fruit	Meat
Crunchy peanut butter	Salted items
Cornmeal or flour	
Other birdseed	
Rolled oats	

Red-bellied
woodpecker at
suet feeder

BACKYARD TIP

Add another sugar-water feeder in late summer when migration increases. This will help keep feisty males from fighting for space.

Sugar Water *101*

Make this the year you attract hummingbirds
(or increase their traffic) in your yard.

The Recipe

If you haven't memorized the recipe yet, then now
is the time. Combine four parts hot water to one
part sugar. Mix it up until it's completely dissolved.
Once it cools to room temperature, it's ready.

To Boil or Not to Boil

Using really hot water will usually suffice.
However, if you plan on making extra sugar
water to store in the fridge or you have so-so
water quality, then it's best to boil.

Honey Do or Honey Don't?

Some people like to come up with creative ways
to sweeten their sugar water without sugar, and
the most common stand-in is honey. Not only is
honey a bad idea in general, but it can also make
your sugar-water mixture ferment more quickly.
Skip the honey; stick to sugar.

The Red Dye Debate

Even though every bird authority around the
country seems to agree that you don't need
red dye, people still add it to their sugar water.
You may also see companies offering premade

sugar water that is red. If this tempts you, don't
feel bad—but it's time to break this habit once
and for all. You don't need red water to attract
hummingbirds. In fact, it could be bad for the
birds (scientists are still figuring this one out).
Either way, it's not worth the risk.

The Important Extras

Sugar water eventually goes bad, unless you're
lucky enough to have a busy feeder that the
hummingbirds quickly empty. You should be in
the habit of changing it every few days or even
sooner if it's really hot out. Also, don't forget
to clean your feeders occasionally. Mold can
collect, so you want to make sure you're offering
hummingbirds clean, safe water.

DID YOU KNOW?

It's always best to stick with real sugar in
your mix. Say no to sugar substitutes.

Feeders *for All*

You can never have enough bird feeders. Learn about the different types available, and make plans to add a new one to your yard.

Hopper

The classic hopper usually has four sides, and it's common to find one in the shape of a house or a barn. Sometimes you can even find options with suet feeders on either end. While it typically doesn't deter squirrels, it does offer a surefire way to offer black oil sunflower seeds to birds of all sizes.

Tray

These types of feeders can either hang or sit atop legs on the ground. In both cases they are completely open, so birds have a big space to land and eat. Tray feeders are often used for larger birds like juncos or mourning doves. Some people who love squirrels even put out their corncobs on tray feeders.

Thistle

Often a tube-shaped feeder, thistle feeders hold the special thistle (Nyjer) seed, which goldfinches love. Some thistle feeders are a simple mesh bag, while others are sturdier. You can even get some that are several feet long, holding dozens of goldfinches at a time.

Tube

If it's not a thistle feeder, other tube feeders have larger holes for seed from sunflowers and safflowers. If you want to deter squirrels, look for tube feeders that have a weighted contraption that closes off seed access when larger birds or squirrels land.

Suet

You can find more than half a dozen suet feeders on the market, including the classic cage design or the cage attached to a vertical wooden platform, giving woodpeckers a better way to perch with their tails.

Baltimore oriole at fruit feeder

Log

You can't get thriftier than taking an old log and drilling holes in the side. These holes are perfect for suet or straight peanut butter. Plus, the log gives woodpeckers and other birds a built-in perch.

Peanut

It's usually shaped like a tube, but you can also find peanut feeders in round, wreath shapes. These feeders have large holes, and the birds (and sometimes squirrels) have to work to get the peanuts out.

Sugar Water

This feeder should be pretty self-explanatory. Look for one in a few standard shapes, and it's for those glorious little fliers we call hummingbirds. Keep in mind that a second sugar-water feeder (usually in an orange color) also attracts orioles and other birds.

Fruit

You can find a handful of other feeders on the market, including those that hold fruit like grapes, jelly, oranges and apples. These are great feeders to experiment with, especially in spring and fall, when you'll see the most migrants.

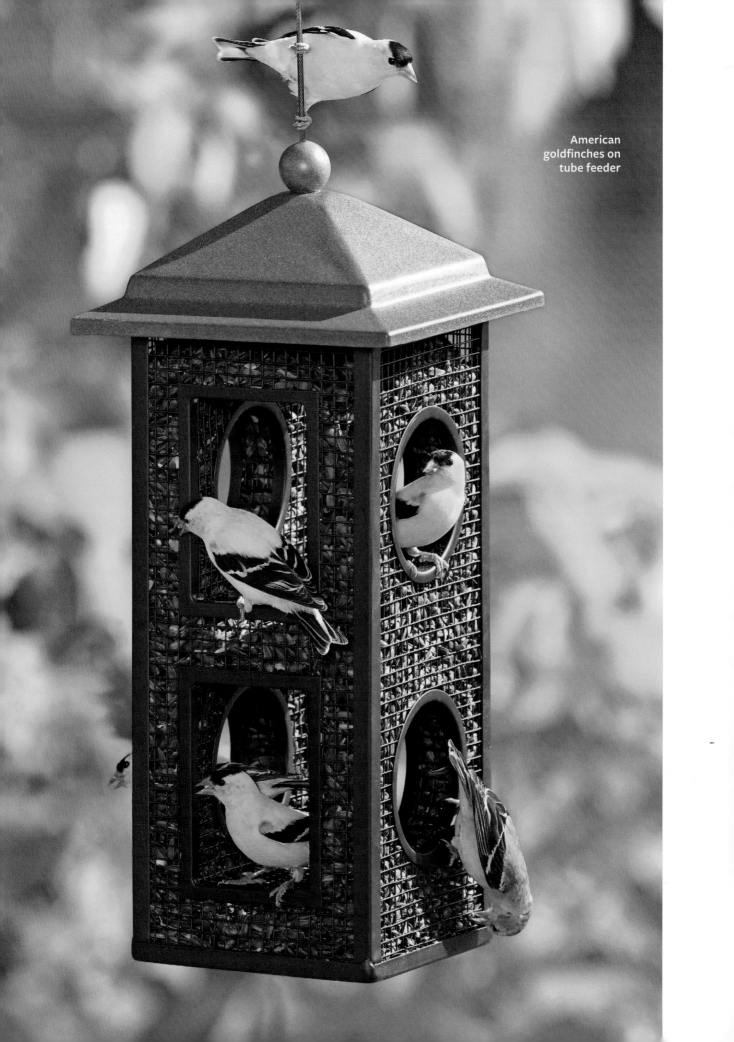

American goldfinches on tube feeder

KEEP 'EM CLEAN

Don't forget to clean your birdhouses, too. Late winter is a good time to prep them for new spring arrivals.

Cleaning *Tips*

Keep the birds in your backyard happy and healthy with these tricks.

More Is Better

Crowded spaces can quickly lead to messy surroundings. This is true in many aspects of life, and it's also true for birds. If you have a single feeder constantly being mobbed by visitors, then maybe it's time to put out another one. This will instantly alleviate all the traffic going to a single source, and it'll help keep your feeding space cleaner longer.

After the Rain

No one likes to eat soggy food, and birds, too, will avoid food that has been out in the rain. Even when it dries, the food is usually moldy, a potential hazard. If you can, set your feeders up under a protected area, away from the rain and damp. If this isn't an option, then be sure to clean them out after the rain.

Good Storage

The seed you use is only as good as your storage method. Let's face it—feeding birds is an investment. That's why it's worth spending some time and effort to come up with a good seed storage solution. Ideally, you'll store your seeds in a sealed container, away from mice, squirrels and other critters. This will keep your area tidy and birds healthy.

Power of Bleach

A good rule of thumb is to clean your feeders at least once with every new season. (An exception is hummingbird feeders, which should be cleaned every week or two during the height of the season.) All you need is a little bit of bleach to give them a good cleaning. Scrub with a mixture of 10 parts water to 1 part bleach. Rinse well.

CLEANING TIPS FROM READERS

The easiest way to clean a birdhouse is by first soaking the inside with water using a spray bottle. Then I just scrape out the old nesting materials.

Tom Kovach
PARK RAPIDS, MINNESOTA

Here's an easy way to make your birdbath sparkle. Toss a handful of sand into the basin and scrub it with a clean brush. The grit helps grind away residue.

Marilyn Clancy
ENGLEWOOD, FLORIDA

I could never get my hummingbird feeders completely clean until I tried this technique. Place a few uncooked navy beans in the feeder with some water, and then gently shake. Hard-to-reach crevices come clean.

Lynn Ray
GREENUP, ILLINOIS

Keep *Food Fresh*

Storing bulk seed the right way saves time and money.

THE MORE BIRDS that find and return to your feeders, the more often you need to fill them. To keep up with demand, it makes sense to buy birdseed in bulk! Stocking up during a sale saves you money, plus it cuts down on your trips to the store, which saves you time. It's a win for you and the birds, but it's important to keep excess food fresh and free of rodent and insect infestations. Luckily, it's easy to manage your bulk food with these simple tips.

Inspect for Dust
It begins at the store. When you're shopping for seeds, avoid picking up dusty bags. The food has likely been sitting there for a while, and it could be close to expiring.

Go for Hulls
Buy seeds with hulls, like black oil sunflower seeds. They stay fresh longer, especially in the heat of summer. Birds don't mind the extra work!

Black oil sunflower seeds

Keep It Cool
Store bird food in a cool, dark place. "Then it will be good for a long time," says Emma Greig, project leader at the Cornell Lab of Ornithology's Project FeederWatch. When it's hot out, "keep bird food in the basement, or buy less quantity in the summer," she says.

Store in an Airtight Container
This is critical to keep out moths and other insects. Once your batch is infested, the whole lot has got to go. Try a large plastic tub or a metal garbage can with a tight lid. And don't worry about any air captured in the container. Emma says it is not a problem.

Try a Sniff Test
Before you refill feeders, give the food a quick sniff. Spoiled seed smells a little off, and if the scent is unappealing to you, it's almost guaranteed the birds will look for their next meal elsewhere.

Freshen Up Feeders
One way to keep the seeds in your feeders from spoiling is by washing the feeders frequently with soap and water. Rinse well, dry and fill with fresh food.

Freeze for Longer Life
Emma estimates that seeds will keep for up to one year if you freeze them. Either toss the whole bag into a chest freezer or separate seeds into smaller portions and seal in freezer-safe storage bags.

Frequent Your Feeders
Take note of what's happening at your feeders. If seed levels in one feeder are declining while another remains full, try refreshing the untouched seed. It may have spoiled—or the birds that ate the seed may have moved on.

ELIMINATE WASTE

Use a small scoop, such as a pitcher, funnel or measuring cup, that lets you easily pour seed into a feeder without spilling.

CHAPTER 4

Gardening
for Birds

*It's never been easier
to create a space that's
irresistible to birds. Put
your green thumb to use
and attract new species.*

Best Plants
for Birds

Use these "Sweet 16" seasonal lists to attract different species year-round.

A LOT OF FLOWERS, shrubs and trees are multitaskers. They adorn your backyard with interesting textures, bright colors and delicious scents while they attract all kinds of winged creatures. To entice birds, butterflies and helpful insects all year, you've got to have the right plants. Use this guide with lists of 16 favorites for each season to make sure you give the birds and other creatures what they need most.

Indigo bunting
in Snowdrift
crabapple tree

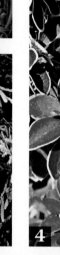

1 American bittersweet

CELASTRUS SCANDENS, ZONES 3 TO 8
Bittersweet's showy orange berries are a favorite of more than a dozen bird species. Growing up to 30 feet tall, this vigorous grower gives ample shelter and offers its seeds to hungry birds in the cold months. You'll need at least one male plant for every five females plants to get fruit.

2 American cranberry-bush viburnum

VIBURNUM TRILOBUM, ZONES 2 TO 7
A boon to gardeners and wildlife alike, this shrub grows 8 to 10 feet tall and wide. Abundant tart red berries appear in summer and stay until late winter, providing both shots of backyard color and food for birds. Plants do best in sun to partial shade and in moist, well-draining soil.

3 Arborvitae

THUJA OCCIDENTALIS, ZONES 3 TO 7
This tree is dense, with a pyramidal shape and clusters of small seed-bearing cones. It has a classic conifer look, offering generous cover for birds. Another plus: You have plenty of cultivars to choose from.

4 Barberry

BERBERIS SPECIES, ZONES 3 TO 8
This shrub is grown for its foliage and will provide much-needed shelter for birds in winter. For the best results in color and fruit, grow in full sun. Barberry will attract gray catbirds, northern mockingbirds and more. This plant is invasive in some states, so do your homework first.

5 Beautyberry

CALLICARPA SPECIES, ZONES 5 TO 8
Beautyberry is a real showstopper in autumn. Its fall fruit lasts well into winter—or until the birds devour the last bunches of bright-purple berries. Beautyberry is a fast-growing shrub that will reach about 4 feet in height.

6 Black chokeberry

ARONIA MELANOCARPA, ZONES 3 TO 9

A lovely and low-maintenance shrub year-round, this chokeberry develops bluish-black fruit that attracts songbirds in fall and winter. Plants grow to be 3 to 6 feet tall and up to 10 feet wide; they do best in sun or part shade and in moist, well-draining soil.

7 Blue spruce

PICEA PUNGENS, ZONES 2 TO 8

Birds love the thick branches and prickly needles that provide winter shelter. The cones produce seed for food. This tree will do best in full sun and will grow up to 60 feet tall.

8 Boxwood

BUXUS SPECIES, ZONES 4 TO 9

Often used for hedges and topiaries, this dense evergreen shrub is covered in masses of green or variegated foliage and thrives in partial shade. Its density makes it a favorite of birds for winter cover. Many slow-growing cultivars reach just 5 feet or less.

9 Firethorn

PYRACANTHA COCCINEA, ZONES 5 TO 9

Looking for beauty in your backyard beyond fall? The firethorn is right for you. Firethorn has glossy green foliage for most of the year, but it's the compact bunches of pea-size berries that get all the attention.

10 Hawthorn

CRATAEGUS, ZONES 3 TO 9

Commonly used as a border tree in backyard landscapes, hawthorn is a haven for birds looking for nesting and perching sites. The tree thrives in full sun and grows to be 20 to 45 feet tall.

11 Hemlock

TSUGA, ZONES 4 TO 8

Hemlock trees are shade-tolerant, especially when they're young, and are popular for hedges. One variety in particular, Cole's Prostrate, has a weeping look with a low, spreading habit and cascading branches. It provides dense shelter for ground-feeding birds like towhees and juncos.

12 Holly
ILEX SPECIES, ZONES 5 TO 9
This winter classic is practically a necessity for bird lovers. Its beautiful green foliage supplies winter protection for flying visitors, and its bright berries are nourishing. Different species range from small bushes to 60-foot trees.

13 Red chokeberry
ARONIA ARBUTIFOLIA, ZONES 4 TO 9
Growing 6 to 10 feet high, this resilient shrub does well even in poor soil, tolerating wet and dry conditions. It has small white or reddish blooms in spring, glossy foliage in summer and bright-red berries in fall and early winter.

14 Serviceberry
AMELANCHIER SPECIES, ZONES 3 TO 9
These small trees or shrubs provide four seasons of interest in just about any landscape. The berries draw northern mockingbirds, brown thrashers, northern flickers, downy woodpeckers and more species later in the year.

15 Sumac
RHUS SPECIES, ZONES 3 TO 10
Sumac is a durable shrub or small tree that's attractive year-round. In winter, it boasts spikes of red fruit that are an excellent source of nutrition for winter residents.

16 Winterberry
ILEX VERTICILLATA, ZONES 3 TO 9
Few deciduous shrubs are as showy in winter as winterberry. It drops its leaves in fall, so nothing detracts from the brilliance of the red berries. Many gardeners find winterberry a must for cold-weather landscaping, and it's easy to see why. You'll love the colorful fruit, and the birds will love you for growing it.

SPRING

1 Bachelor's buttons
CENTAUREA CYANUS, ANNUAL
Also known as cornflowers, bachelor's buttons bloom in late spring through summer. The wide purple and bluish flowers look like buttons. For spring blooms, be sure to sow seeds in early fall. Some likely visitors are finches, buntings and sparrows.

2 Baptisia
BAPTISIA, ZONES 3 TO 9
These pretty flowers look like pea blossoms. A single plant can grow to be 5 feet high and 2 feet wide. Baptisia sprouts interesting seedpods that will bring in the birds.

3 Buckeye
AESCULUS SPECIES, ZONES 3 TO 8
If you're looking to add charm to your landscape, plant a buckeye shrub or small tree. The leaves of red buckeye are distinctive, and the showy red flowers attract hummingbirds while providing shelter for other birds in spring.

4 Butterfly weed
ASCLEPIAS TUBEROSA, ZONES 3 TO 9
Not solely for butterflies, this plant is truly multipurpose. Hummingbirds, too, love its nectar, and goldfinches and orioles are among the birds that use the silky seed down as nesting material.

5 Camellia
CAMELLIA, ZONES 6 TO 11
This popular evergreen flowers in the fall, winter or early spring, depending on the variety. Ideal for landscaping, it has lovely rose-shaped blooms, usually in red, pink or white. Birds will appreciate the shrub during nesting season. Expect camellia to be anywhere from 3 to 20 feet high.

6 Cherry
PRUNUS SPECIES, ZONES 3 TO 9
Beautiful pink blooms open in spring, and small red or black fruit appears in summer. The birds will welcome the shelter and eat up the berries in summer. Cherry trees come in dwarf varieties if you don't want a large one.

7 Columbine

AQUILEGIA, ZONES 3 TO 9

The blooms of columbine are truly stunning. Hummingbirds and butterflies love them! Remove spent blossoms to encourage more to form into early summer. Avoid fertilizing too much, which results in fewer blooms.

8 Foxglove

DIGITALIS, ZONES 3 TO 10

Foxglove is a short-lived perennial or a biennial. Its tubular, bell-shaped blooms come in a variety of colors: apricot, pink, golden brown, coppery rose and more. Hummingbirds flock to these flowers.

9 Fuchsia

FUCHSIA SPECIES, ANNUAL TO ZONE 8

Fuchsia's showy red, white, pink and purple blooms will capture your heart and bring in the hummingbirds. There are more than 100 kinds, from low-growing dwarfs to upright varieties. Most plants are 6 to 24 inches. Fuchsia grows best in partial shade.

10 Lupine

LUPINUS PERENNIS, ZONES 3 TO 9

Lupine blooms from late spring to early summer. It grows about 3 to 4 feet tall and produces spires of blooms that look like pea blossoms. Lupine will do best in full sun to partial shade.

11 Phlox

PHLOX, ZONES 3 TO 9

These old-fashioned beauties attract hummingbirds and butterflies as soon as they start blooming in spring. The flowers, prized for their scent, come in many colors, sizes and bloom times. Most varieties prefer full sun.

12 Pine

PINUS, MOST ZONES, CHECK SPECIES

Pines provide the shelter and nesting space that spring birds need. Plant trees any time from spring to fall in moist, well-draining soil. But beware: Some pine trees can grow to be 75 feet tall.

13 Redbud

CERCIS SPECIES, ZONES 4 TO 10

Redbud's blooms attract hummingbirds and butterflies, as well as pollinating insects that benefit your backyard. The seeds appeal to chickadees, goldfinches and others, and woodpeckers and nuthatches love the insects in the bark.

14 Red-hot poker

KNIPHOFIA, ZONES 5 TO 9

It's easy to see why this plant is also called a torch lily. Birds love this stately flower, which changes in color from yellow at the base to bright red at the tip. Depending on the cultivar, it will bloom in late spring to autumn, and attract flocks of hummingbirds along the way.

15 Rhododendron

RHODODENDRON SPECIES, ZONES 4 TO 9

Plant rhododendron in a lightly shaded area with protection from winter sun and winds. Moist, acidic soil that drains well will help it thrive. Rhododendron offers ample shelter and enticing nectar.

16 Viburnum

VIBURNUM SPECIES, ZONES 3 TO 10

This bush draws a variety of birds with nesting space and summer-to-winter fruit. Viburnum is among the most popular ornamental shrubs and small trees because it's beautiful, versatile and easy to grow.

Black-capped chickadee in rhododendron

1 Bee balm

MONARDA, ZONES 3 TO 9

If you want to lure hummingbirds and butterflies, this easy-to-grow perennial is a good selection. Its bright colors and nectar-filled blooms attract a variety of pretty fliers. The plant grows up to 4 feet tall and starts flowering in midsummer.

2 Black-eyed Susan

RUDBECKIA SPECIES, ZONES 3 TO 9

Birds adore this garden classic. The traditional black-eyed Susan has a dark center and bright-yellow petals, but now there are a few new color combos to choose from. Grow in full sun to light shade for blooms from summer through autumn. House finches, chickadees and American goldfinches will feed on the seed heads.

3 Blanket flower

GAILLARDIA X GRANDIFLORA, ZONES 3 TO 9

Blanket flower will bloom all summer, showing off its vibrant red and yellow blooms. The plant is generally 2 to 3 feet tall and does best in full sun.

4 Coralbells

HEUCHERA, ZONES 3 TO 9

Rich, fertile soil is best and partial shade ideal for this handsome plant. Coralbells are valued for their colorful, often purple foliage. In late spring, the plant sends up attractive, long-lasting wands of tiny flowers that hummingbirds love.

5 Coreopsis

COREOPSIS SPECIES, ZONES 3 TO 11

Nectar-rich blooms appeal to hummingbirds and butterflies, while the seeds provide food for sparrows, chickadees, finches and other seed-eating birds. Plant drought-tolerant coreopsis in full sun.

6 Cosmos

COSMOS BIPINNATUS, ANNUAL

Birds can't resist these pinwheel-shaped blooms nestled in feathery foliage. Grow single or double cultivars in full sun, and you'll have colorful flowers and seeds from summer through fall.

7 Flowering tobacco

NICOTIANA ALATA, ANNUAL

For a no-fuss way to liven up your garden with hummingbirds and butterflies, plant flowering tobacco. The stems rise from a rosette of leaves and are covered with star-shaped flowers in shades of pink, red, maroon, lavender, white, yellow and even green.

8 Liatris

LIATRIS SPICATA, ZONES 3 TO 9

Also called gayfeather or blazing star, this flower shines in late spring through summer. It attracts hummingbirds to its spikes of lavender, rose or white blossoms. American goldfinches, tufted titmice and other seed eaters savor its seed heads.

9 Penstemon

PENSTEMON SPECIES, ZONES 3 TO 10

Hummingbirds love these red, purple, blue, pink and white flowers on plants that reach up to 4 feet and will bloom profusely for most or all of the summer. Full sun and well-draining soil are ideal; damp or rich soil makes it rot.

10 Primrose

PRIMULA VULGARIS, ZONES 4 TO 8

English primrose is a favorite of hummingbirds, butterflies and bees because of its alluring fragrance in early summer. It's generally a profuse bloomer, doing best in partial shade.

11 Purple coneflower

ECHINACEA SPECIES, ZONES 3 TO 10

The large, showy blooms of coneflowers will attract birds, butterflies and bees. Plant bare-root perennials in spring, or plant container-grown specimens any time during the growing season. Cut back half your coneflowers in early summer to delay flowering and prolong overall bloom time.

12 Salvia

SALVIA SPECIES, ZONES 4 TO 9

Annual salvia is a garden favorite, but don't forget the perennials. Loose flower spires reach heights from 1 to 5 feet. The blooms come in bright shades of red, maroon, purple and indigo—and hummingbirds love them!

13 Stokesia

STOKESIA LAEVIS, ZONES 5 TO 9

Blooming from early summer until fall, stokesia boasts 3- to 5-inch-wide blue, lavender or pink blooms with ragged-toothed petals around a creamy center. Regular deadheading will extend blooms and ensure plenty of bird activity.

14 Trumpet vine

CAMPSIS RADICANS, ZONES 4 TO 9

Trumpet vine blooms are orange-red in color and tubular in shape, making them a favorite of hummingbirds. Surprisingly, this vine can grow to be 40 feet tall. Plant it in full sun.

15 Yarrow

ACHILLEA SPECIES, ZONES 3 TO 10

Flattened clusters of tiny flowers attract hummingbirds and butterflies, while the seeds of yarrow appeal to many songbirds.

16 Zinnia

ZINNIA, ANNUAL

An old-fashioned favorite, zinnias are best loved for their long-lasting blooms that require minimal care. The flowers will attract hummingbirds and butterflies in the heat of summer. And without deadheading, zinnias will bloom into fall.

AUTUMN

1 Aster

ASTER SPECIES, ZONES 3 TO 8

The aster brings an explosion of color to the end of the growing season, a guaranteed lure for fall butterflies. From miniature alpine plants to giants up to 6 feet tall, it will brighten up fall in your backyard. Plant early in the season in northern states so it can get established before winter.

2 Crabapple

MALUS SPECIES, ZONES 2 TO 9

These highly decorative flowering trees produce small fruits that attract more than 20 bird species but are especially favored by cedar waxwings, robins and northern cardinals. Varieties tend to be 10 to 25 feet tall and grow best in full sun.

3 Dogwood

CORNUS SPECIES, ZONES 2 TO 8

Bursting with berries, this garden favorite feeds bluebirds, cardinals, robins and dozens of other backyard birds during the colder months. Dogwoods do best in full sun to partial shade and prefer moist soil.

4 Elderberry

SAMBUCUS SPECIES, ZONES 3 TO 9

A luxurious shrub with long, drooping branches, elderberry produces flat white clusters of flowers that turn into purple berries in late summer. The fruit is relished by gray catbirds, robins, bluebirds and many other backyard songbirds.

5 Fountain grass

PENNISETUM ALOPECUROIDES, ZONES 5 TO 9

With full tufts of fuzzy flower spikes that turn into natural birdseed, fountain grass seems to be heaven-sent. One or more of its many varieties, which reach 2 to 5 feet, will add charm to your backyard wildlife habitat.

6 Four-o'clocks

MIRABILIS JALAPA, ANNUAL

The blooms of four-o'clocks earn their name, opening in midafternoon and fading before sunrise. The nectar-rich flowers are a favorite evening stop for hummingbirds and butterflies.

7 Goldenrod

SOLIDAGO SPECIES, ZONES 3 TO 9

All it takes is a few goldenrod plants to lighten up your garden in late summer and provide birds a continual food source. Give the plants plenty of room to spread. They won't disappoint, especially as many other plants fade.

8 Grape

VITIS, ZONES 2 TO 9

This high-sugar fruit provides lots of energy for birds. The woody deciduous vines grow up to 30 feet long, thrive in full sun, and produce late-summer and autumn fruit in a variety of sizes and flavors, some of which are unpalatable to humans.

9 Joe Pye weed

EUTROCHIUM PURPUREUM, ZONES 4 TO 9

Grow Joe Pye weed in average to moist soil. It offers a great supply of seed that birds will love. Pinch back early in the season to grow shorter plants and boost flower production.

10 Mahonia

MAHONIA, ZONES 5 TO 11

This evergreen shrub has spiny-edged leaves and, in late summer and fall, bears clusters of blue-black berries. Various species grow from 1 to 12 feet in full sun to light shade.

11 Marigold

TAGETES, ANNUAL

For brilliant and lasting color, look no further. Marigolds are tough garden plants that bloom and attract birds through fall, with varieties growing from 6 inches to 3 feet tall.

12 Mountain ash

SORBUS SPECIES, ZONES 2 TO 7

A good choice for small landscapes, this medium-size tree boasts spectacular yellow and red fall foliage. The orange fruit attracts flocks of cedar waxwings, robins, gray catbirds, thrashers, eastern bluebirds and at least a dozen other bird species.

13 Nasturtium

TROPAEOLUM MAJUS, ANNUAL

Nasturtiums will bloom from early summer straight through until frost. Extremely low-maintenance plants, they have funnel-shaped flowers and large, veined leaves. Hummingbirds and butterflies will stop to visit the blooms, and it's also worth noting that all parts of the plant are edible for humans!

14 Rugosa rose

ROSA RUGOSA, ZONES 2 TO 8

Love roses but hate the hassle? This fast-growing variety flourishes anywhere without the fuss. Rugosa roses handle poor soil conditions, from sandy to salty, and produce bright rose hips that attract countless birds.

15 Sedum

SEDUM SPECIES, ZONES 3 TO 10

Just when your other plants begin their fall decline, Autumn Joy sedum will take the spotlight with its brightening star-shaped blooms. Most sedums are hardy in all but the coldest climates. The late-autumn seed heads attract birds, including finches and chickadees, so don't cut them back until spring.

16 Sunflower

HELIANTHUS ANNUUS, ANNUAL

Sunflowers are dependable bird magnets. Cultivars range anywhere from 2 to 15 feet tall and are mainly yellow, although some varieties are red or brown. In early autumn, this stately beauty attracts all kinds of seed eaters.

Gardening for Birds
Seasonal Checklist

Northern cardinal

Tufted titmouse

WINTER

- Peruse seed catalogs and *Birds & Blooms* to decide what wildlife magnets you'd like to purchase for the coming growing season.
- Ring in the New Year by starting a garden journal that chronicles Mother Nature's activities in your yard, from what's growing to who's visiting and what the weather's like.
- After big storms, gently brush snow off berry- and seed-bearing plants to make the food more accessible to birds. Be careful not to shake; you don't want to damage the plants.
- Design a new garden that's geared toward attracting birds and butterflies. Be sure to incorporate plants that are useful year-round, whether for food or shelter.

SPRING

- Scour garden centers for plants wildlife love. Refer to the seasonal plant profiles here, as well as plant tags, for info on varieties that are especially attractive to birds and butterflies.
- Prepare gardens and plant annuals, perennials, trees and shrubs that will attract wildlife. Remember to include those that offer edibles and refuge.
- Remove and compost seed heads, dried foliage and any other perennial remnants that stayed in the garden over winter. The birds have likely picked the seed heads clean.
- Prune summer-flowering shrubs before growth begins, including bluebeard, summersweet and rose of Sharon, to encourage bushy growth and plenty of blooms for hummers and butterflies to enjoy.

American goldfinch

Ruby-throated hummingbird

SUMMER

- Attract beneficial insects to your garden, along with the birds that eat them. Sweet alyssum, creeping thyme, veronica, bugleweed, lavender and yarrow are among the plants that attract parasitic wasps, lady beetles, lacewings and other insects that feed on garden pests.

- Have thistles in your garden? Stop yourself from pulling them out. American goldfinches wait for the thistles to mature and use the down to build their nests.

- Extend hummingbird and butterfly season by filling your garden with long-blooming nectar plants, such as zinnias, agastache, salvia and blanket flower.

- If your garden has a water feature, make it double as a birdbath by placing a few large rocks around the edge to offer fliers a convenient place to sit and drink.

AUTUMN

- Fall is a good time for planting some small trees and shrubs, such as crabapple and elderberry. These trees attract butterflies and beneficial insects, offer fruit for birds, and provide shelter and shade year-round. Check with your local nursery or extension office on what to plant this time of year.

- Make sure you have plenty of salvias, asters, cardinal flowers and mums in your garden for fall fliers.

- Many backyard shrubs and trees, including mountain ash, viburnum and cotoneaster, are laden with birds' favorite berries. Don't have these? Plant one or two for next year.

- During late-autumn garden cleanup, let healthy, pest-free perennials stand. They add beauty to the winter landscape, provide food for birds and are winter homes for many good bugs.

BEST FOR BIRDS

Look for sunflower varieties that produce an ample supply of seeds for birds to gobble up. Try Mammoth Gray Stripe, Paul Bunyan and Aztec Gold.

Grow Your *Own Birdseed*

Native sunflowers attract beautiful birds, prized pollinators and important insects.

WHETHER YOU'RE already a dedicated caretaker of backyard feeders or brand-new to birding, it's always a good idea to kick it up a notch! Plant native sunflowers to attract and feed your beloved birds, build a healthier habitat and make your space easy to manage.

"Anybody, anywhere they live, can support the birds they love by growing native plants," says Tod Winston, program manager for the National Audubon Society's Plants for Birds program. Sunflowers are simple—it doesn't take much for their seeds to take root. Provide them with plenty of sun and a spot in a patio pot, raised bed or garden, and you'll soon have a crop of flourishing flowers.

Start Here

Check out the National Audubon Society's Native Plants Database or consult local native nurseries to select an ideal species. Plant your sunflower seeds in late spring. The soil must be warm and dry, with no possibility of frost.

Sunflower seeds need a soil temperature of about 50 degrees Fahrenheit to sprout. Measure with a thermometer or go with your gut. To test the soil moisture, grab a handful and squeeze. The soil is too wet if it sticks together and doesn't crumble. Once conditions are just right, plant the seeds up to 1 inch deep, with about 12 inches between each seed. They'll need about six to eight hours of sunlight each day.

Make an Impact

"The more people who plant native plants in their yard, the more resilient birds are going to be in the face of climate change and in the face of continuing loss of habitat," Tod says. He adds that nearly 41% of all migratory songbird populations in North America are declining.

Sunflowers also benefit many pollinators, caterpillars and birds. Their compound flower heads are packed with pollen, and these bright beauties host more than 70 species of native moth and butterfly caterpillars. That's a big deal because one nest of Carolina chickadee chicks may eat up to 9,000 caterpillars before fledging. Plus, 90% of land birds feed insects to chicks, so it's important to protect those local populations. As a bonus, migrating birds love the seeds because they're high-fat fuel for their journeys south.

Grow Related Natives

If you're seeking some variety to beautify your backyard, consider planting other natives from the aster family, including coneflowers, tickseed and black- and brown-eyed Susans.

SUNFLOWER LOVERS
These birds can't resist the seedy snacks.

Cardinals	Sparrows
Grosbeaks	Buntings
Chickadees	Juncos
Titmice	Redpolls
Crows	Towhees
Jays	Woodpeckers
Finches	Wrens
Nuthatches	Pine siskins

Plant a Buffet of *Safflower*

Cultivating this annual will delight cardinals, chickadees, jays and more.

MOVE OVER, SUNFLOWERS—there's a new seed in town. Safflower is easy to grow and provides your feathered friends with first-rate food.

The first time I found sprouting safflowers under my bird feeder in spring, I thought they were sunflowers. The seedlings look a lot alike, with each stem sporting a pair of smooth green ovals. But the next leaves, the true leaves, told a different tale. They were deep, glossy green with sawtooth edges. So I was puzzled at the new sprouts.

Then I remembered I'd added safflower seeds to my feeder menu earlier that winter. The cardinals loved them. The seeds must either have fallen out of the feeder or been cached by jays. Either way, I had a little plantation going, and I couldn't wait to see the end results.

Time to Grow

Unlike sunflowers, these seedlings take their time. They put up a rosette of leaves and then stall for a few weeks. Meanwhile, an incredible taproot is growing underground, snaking 4 feet deep or more in a single season.

With a root like that, you'd think this would be a hardy perennial. But safflower's an annual: After the first hard frost in fall, it dies.

Safflower needs a growing season of 100 days or longer to produce seeds, about the same as winter squash. If you can grow pumpkins, you can grow safflower.

Perfect Partners

Even if the birds don't plant it for you, safflower is simple to grow. Just poke some kernels from your seed mix into the ground in spring, about the time you notice sunflowers starting to sprout. Plant them about an inch deep in a sunny spot.

Safflower leaves get spiny as the plant matures. To save your fingers, grow the plant in a casual bed with some blue larkspur, bachelor's buttons, cosmos, marigolds and other easy-care, self-sowing annuals where it can take care of itself.

The fluffy flowers bloom just in time to catch the last wave of butterflies—migrating monarchs, skippers, sulfurs and other nectar seekers still on the wing.

Once upon a time, most safflower blooms were a rich shade of orange, so deep the petals were used for dye. But today's varieties were developed for seed production, not color, so the blossoms may be orange, pale yellow, buttery gold or even red.

Keep the Birds Fed

Each flower holds just a few dozen seeds, but each branching, 2- to 3-foot-tall plant holds lots of flowers. By autumn, their ripening seeds will be packed with protein.

Even a small planting can keep cardinals, jays, chickadees, titmice, finches, native sparrows and doves investigating all fall and winter.

Come springtime, you're likely to find some volunteers from seeds that got buried under the snow or fallen leaves. Want more? Just reach for the bag of birdseed.

—*Sally Roth*

Cardinals
love this
seed

Lettuce for *Finches*

Discover why this easy-to-grow seed will keep birds happy for months.

Female American goldfinch

I'VE OFTEN wondered why birdseed growers don't investigate more varieties of seeds for commercial sale. After all, I see how birds flock to my yard and garden to eat the seeds right off my perennials and annuals.

Sure, nobody wants a feeder mix packed with genuine thistle, dandelion and teasel seeds. But what about, say, lettuce?

Ready to Bolt

Lettuce is easy to grow and full of seeds, and it's not a problem if the extras happen to sprout beneath the feeder. It's also such a powerful temptation to goldfinches that the cheery black-and-yellow fliers once went by the nickname "lettuce birds."

It's not salad that the finches are seeking. Although goldfinches may nibble tender young lettuce leaves in spring, the big payoff comes when the plants bolt and go to seed.

That's when finches come flocking. Even a single stem of lettuce seeds can attract a dozen finches; a larger patch can bring in an unbelievable multitude.

When I counted 200 sunny yellow goldfinches at one time in my first lettuce plantation—which was nothing more than a single 6-foot row in my garden that had gone to seed—I knew I'd have to make the plant a staple in my bird-friendly yard.

Turn the Heat Up

Most advice about growing lettuce focuses on getting more greens, not more seeds. At the first sign of bolting, which usually happens when summer heats up, we yank out the plants, wait until the weather cools and start a new crop.

What a waste! As far as finches are concerned, that flowering stem is the promise of good things to come. Pull out such precious plants? I don't think so. That's why I now plant lettuce in my flower beds, where it can live out its more natural life among cosmos, bachelor's buttons, sunflowers and other self-sowing annuals. The finches love them all.

Now I look at my garden lettuce differently and encourage others to do the same. When my crop begins to bolt in summer heat, I don't mourn the loss of my salad greens. I think, "Oh, boy! Get ready for goldfinches!"
—*Sally Roth*

Bolted
lettuces
with leeks

SALAD OR SEEDS?

Pruning

FOR SALAD Cut off the flowering stems as they form, so the plant produces more leaves.

FOR SEED Let the flowering stems stretch for the skies.

Planting

FOR SALAD Plant in tidy rows.

FOR SEED Scatter the seeds willy-nilly for a casual patch, or sprinkle seeds among your cosmos and other annuals that self-sow.

Thinning

FOR SALAD Thin seedlings to provide generous, regular spacing that will give each plant room to grow.

FOR SEED Simply let seedlings duke it out for elbow room. Some will become larger plants than others, but all will produce abundantly.

Watering

FOR SALAD Water generously.

FOR SEED Let the soil dry out between rain showers to encourage flowering rather than leafy growth.

Soil

FOR SALAD Plant in fertilized soil.

FOR SEED Plant in any well-drained garden soil. Lettuce plants will get enough nourishment through their deep taproots to produce copious seeds, even if leafy growth is scanty.

Naturally *Native*

Plant native grasses and watch your yard come alive with birds and butterflies.

ALL-SEASON APPEAL Native grasses offer nesting material in spring, a treat for caterpillars in summer and seeds for birds in fall and winter.

ORNAMENTAL GRASSES are full of life. They sway in the wind, bow beneath snow and rustle with gentle music all their own throughout the seasons.

Keep an eye on those graceful clumps and you'll see life of another kind, too. Birds and butterflies love them. Native sparrows, finches and other small birds forage for seeds from grasses in the garden, just as they do in the wild. And more than 100 butterfly species, especially skippers, use certain grasses as host plants.

With so many kinds of ornamental grasses on the market, and new ones joining them every year, how's a gardener to know which ones are best for birds and butterflies? It's simple, really. Go native!

Benefits to Birds

Birds visit all North American native grasses, thanks to the bounty of nutritious morsels on the plumes, spikes or sprays. For juncos, native sparrows, buntings and other seed-eating birds, it doesn't matter what part of the country the grass is originally from.

Many natives, such as switchgrass, big bluestem and Indian grass, are already garden favorites as ornamentals, both in their original form and in variations like the Heavy Metal cultivar, which is a cool blue-gray.

Don't expect to see your ornamental grasses bowing under a flock of feeding goldfinches, though. Instead, look for finches, native sparrows, juncos, doves and other birds on the ground beneath the plants in fall and winter, stretching for overhanging seed heads or scratching for fallen seeds.

Spring and Summer Appeal

In spring, when nesting season arrives, any and all grasses may be the focus of birds' attention. Dead grass, that is.

Dry grass is lightweight, plentiful, easy to maneuver around and a cinch to collect. Birds aren't fussy about what they use in their nests, as long as it's strong and flexible.

Robins, song sparrows, wrens and other birds use coarse grass blades, such as miscanthus, for the main wall of a nest. The dead leaves of other fine-textured grasses often serve as part of the soft inner circlet that lines the nest.

Grasses come into their glory as summer arrives, and that's when delightful grass skipper butterflies take an interest in them, too. This big subfamily includes about 140 species, all with a definite predilection for grasses as host plants.

So go ahead and add a few grasses to your backyard. Fall is still a good time to plant them. You'll be well on your way to attracting even more birds and butterflies to your space.

9 NATIVE PICKS FOR BIRDS

BIG BLUESTEM (*Andropogon gerardii*)

BLUE GRAMA GRASS (*Bouteloua gracilis*)

INDIAN RICEGRASS (*Achnatherum hymenoides*)

LITTLE BLUESTEM (*Schizachyrium scoparium*)

MUHLY GRASS (*Muhlenbergia spp.*)

NORTHERN SEA OATS (*Chasmanthium latifolium*)

PRAIRIE DROPSEED (*Sporobolus heterolepsis*)

SIDEOATS GRAMA (*Bouteloua curtipendula*)

SWITCHGRASS (*Panicum virgatum*)

When you cut back your ornamental grasses in early spring, pile some of the clippings where you can keep an eye on them. Nest-building birds will soon spot the freebies-for-all.

Baird's sparrow

Wildflowers for *Hummingbirds*

Mimic a natural habitat with native blooms flowing with nectar.

Rufous at
bee balm

1 Red Columbine
AQUILEGIA CANADENSIS, ZONES 3 TO 8
Bell-shaped red and yellow blooms emerge in spring and last until early summer. Grow columbine in full sun to partial shade and in well-draining soil. This wildflower, like many, seeds itself to create a colony of flowering plants for you to adore or share with others.
Why we love it: Hummingbirds love these plants, but deer and rabbits tend to leave columbine alone.

2 Sage
SALVIA SPECIES, ZONES 3 TO 11,
VARIES WITH SPECIES
There's a good chance you're already growing one or more of the 95 North American native salvias. With so many salvia options out there, you'll want to choose one that works in your zone. For example, mealycup salvia (*Salvia farinacea*) is a Texas native hardy in zones 7 to 11 but grown as an annual elsewhere.
Why we love it: These plants, hummingbird magnets, come in several colors. Arizona sage has deep blue flowers, Texas sage has bright red flowers and Gregg's sage has white, pink or red flowers.

3 Cardinal flower
LOBELIA CARDINALIS, ZONES 3 TO 9
Brighten up a summer garden with spikes of scarlet red, white or rose-colored flowers. Watch for butterflies that will also stop by for a visit, while the rabbits will usually pass on by. Add a few touches of blue to the garden with its close relative great blue lobelia (*Lobelia siphilitica*).
Why we love it: Cardinal flowers are ideal for challenging growing conditions, like those in partial shade with moist to wet soil.

4 Anise hyssop
AGASTACHE FOENICULUM, ZONES 4 TO 8
The anise-scented leaves inspired the common name of this summer bloomer. It thrives in full sun or part shade and in well-drained to dry soil. You'll want to give this 2- to 4-foot plant plenty of room to spread because it readily reseeds.
Why we love it: The lavender flowers also attract butterflies and bees, but deer tend to let it be.

5 Bee balm
MONARDA SPECIES, ZONES 3 TO 9
Rows of red or purple tubular flowers top bee balm's 2- to 4-foot stems throughout summer. Grow this vigorous self-seeder in full sun or partial shade, allowing it plenty of room to expand. The leaves are fragrant when crushed and can be used for tea.
Why we love it: Bee balm's blooms attract a lot of backyard wildlife—hummingbirds, butterflies and bees. Plus, the plants grow successfully near black walnut trees.

6 Scarlet gilia
IPOMOPSIS RUBRA, ZONES 5 TO 9, BIENNIAL
Watch this plant transform from a mat of feathery foliage the first year to tall stems with finely dissected leaves and tubular red flowers the second year. Also known as standing cypress or Texas plume, gilia thrives in full sun and well-drained to dry soil.
Why we love it: Scarlet gilia is a biennial that seeds itself, rewarding you with gorgeous flowering plants for many years.

7 Woodland phlox
PHLOX DIVARICATA, ZONES 3 TO 8
Here's one for the shadows. Grow woodland phlox in partial or full shade and moist, well-drained soil. Once established, it tolerates drought but does best if you mulch during hot summer months. To reduce the risk of powdery mildew, trim the stems back after the flowers die off.
Why we love it: The rose, lavender or violet-blue flowers are lightly fragrant.

8 Beardtongue
PENSTEMON SPECIES, ZONES 3 TO 10,
VARIES WITH SPECIES

You'll find native penstemon in every state
(except Hawaii) and Canadian province.
Many varieties bloom in late spring through
early summer while others provide nectar
and color from summer until fall. Most tolerate
drought. Before growing beardtongue, find
one that's native to your area and suited to
your growing conditions.
Why we love it: Red beardtongue (*Penstemon
barbatus*) is valuable to beneficial insects and
attracts large numbers of native bees.

9 Fringed bleeding heart
DICENTRA EXIMIA, ZONES 3 TO 9

You may be surprised to learn this landscape
plant is native to the eastern U.S. It blooms later
than the larger common bleeding heart, which
is native to Asia. The rosy to purplish-red
flowers appear in late spring and continue
through midsummer on 12- to 18-inch plants.
Grow fringed bleeding heart in partial shade
and moist soil for best results.
Why we love it: The fern-like gray-green
leaves stay intact and add interest throughout
the growing season.

10 Lupine
LUPINUS, ZONES 3 TO 8

There are over 200 species of lupines, most of
which are native to North America. You can find
bluebonnets in Texas, annual sky blue and yellow
lupines in California, blue pod lupines in the
Pacific Northwest and British Columbia, and
wild blue lupine throughout much of the country.
Why we love it: While hummingbirds can't get
enough of the flowers, birds and small mammals
eat the seeds. Karner blue and frosted elfin
butterfly larvae feed on the foliage.

Bloomtastic *Trees*

Celebrate the season with one of these special specimens, most of them sized perfectly for small spaces.

Chipping sparrow

1

1 Flowering crabapple

MALUS, ZONES 4 TO 8
SIZE: 6 TO 8 FEET TALL AND WIDE
TO 20 TO 25 FEET TALL AND WIDE

Crabapples are the darlings of cool-climate backyards. Flowers of white, pink or deep crimson transform into dainty fruits in yellow, orange, maroon or red. Try a newer variety to ensure disease- and pest-resistance, and plant in full sun.

Why we love it: We love the diversity! Flowering crabapple tree shapes can be rounded, spreading, upright, vase shaped and even weeping.

2 Magnolia

MAGNOLIA, ZONES 4 TO 9
SIZE: 15 TO 40 FEET TALL AND WIDE

Gorgeous blooms in white, pink, yellow and purple balance like starbursts atop branches that later bear green leaves, some as glossy as lacquer. Plant in full sun to part shade.

Why we love it: There's one for most regions, from the star magnolia (*Magnolia stellata*) in the chilly North to southern and champaca magnolias in the balmy South, and saucer magnolias everywhere in between.

3 Carolina silverbell

HALESIA TETRAPTERA (OR HALESIA CAROLINA)
ZONES 4 TO 8
SIZE: 30 TO 40 FEET TALL, 20 TO 35 FEET WIDE

Almost maintenance-free and able to grow in full sun to full shade, Carolina silverbell needs moist and well-draining, acidic soil. Test your soil for a pH below 7.

Why we love it: Children and adults alike might believe that fairies come by to ring its elegant white or rose-colored, bell-shaped blossoms.

4 Japanese tree lilac

SYRINGA RETICULATA SSP. RETICULATA, ZONES 3 TO 7
SIZE: 20 TO 30 FEET TALL, 15 TO 25 FEET WIDE

Flowering a bit later than other lilacs, this underused tree releases a sweet scent from its cone-shaped panicles of ivory blooms. Sorry, Southerners, but this is a cold-climate choice. Plant in full sun.

Why we love it: It's unusual and grows even in the most difficult places, such as highway medians.

5 Yellowwood
CLADRASTIS KENTUKEA, ZONES 4 TO 8
SIZE: 30 TO 50 FEET TALL AND SLIGHTLY WIDER
Yellowwood's best bloom show occurs every other year with cascading 8- to 14-inch sprays of delicate, fragrant white blossoms. Grow it in full sun. If you live in areas of heavy snow, beware of branches that snap off in winter.
Why we love it: This is a blooming shade tree, and has bark like a beech tree, providing winter interest.

6 Apple serviceberry
AMELANCHIER X GRANDIFLORA, ZONES 4 TO 9
SIZE: 20 TO 25 FEET TALL AND WIDE
Apple serviceberry is just one kind of serviceberry that's perfect for most landscapes, thanks to its moderate size, bird-attracting berries and ability to thrive in sun or partly sunny locations.
Why we love it: It's a special tree with four seasons of beauty: spring blooms that become red-purple edible fruits, green leaves that flush with orange to red fall color, and smooth silver bark that's gorgeous in winter.

7 Eastern redbud
CERCIS CANADENSIS, ZONES 4 TO 9
SIZE: 20 TO 30 FEET TALL, 25 TO 35 FEET WIDE
Dainty rose-purple blossoms dramatically hang from the branches of this North American native well before the heart-shaped leaves appear. Plant in full sun to part shade.
Why we love it: The small size of this tree fits most yards. You can select alternate leaf colors, such as burgundy Forest Pansy or lime-gold The Rising Sun.

ROOM TO GROW Plant your eastern redbud tree in a spot where it has space to spread out, because this spring showstopper is wider than it is tall.

8

8 Japanese flowering cherry
PRUNUS SERRULATA, ZONES 5 TO 8
SIZE: 40 TO 50 FEET TALL AND 25 TO 40 FEET WIDE
You might *ooh* and *aah* every spring at the photos of the cherry tree display in Washington, D.C., but you can plant a flowering show of your own. Choose a spot in full sun.
Why we love it: With the right cultivar, those gorgeous pink or white blooms turn into fruits that common songbirds—especially robins, cardinals and waxwings—crave.

9 Dogwood
CORNUS KOUSA, ZONES 5 TO 8
CORNUS FLORIDA, ZONES 5 TO 9;
SIZE: 20 TO 40 FEET TALL AND WIDE
Flowers of up to 4 inches across grace spring branches of North American and Asian dogwoods. Test your soil pH before planting because dogwood grows and performs best when it's planted in acidic soil in full sun to full shade.

Why we love it: In addition to the graceful spring blooms and fall leaf colors, the super colorful red fruits produced by dogwood are gobbled up by feathered friends.

10 White fringe tree
CHIONANTHUS VIRGINICUS, ZONES 4 TO 9
SIZE: 12 TO 20 FEET TALL AND WIDE
Native from southern Pennsylvania south to Florida and west to Texas, fringe tree bursts onto the spring scene with lightly fragrant strappy white petals. They're held in small groups attached at the top like tassels.
Why we love it: It's the best-kept secret among spring-blooming trees, yet it's one of the most adaptable, thriving in full sun to part shade. Female trees produce blue fruits that birds love.

9

10

CHAPTER 5

Common *Backyard Birds*

Use this handy resource to help identify frequent fliers and learn about their range, nesting habits, diet and more.

BIRD RANGE
MAP KEY

- Winter
- Summer
- Year-Round
- Migration

Bluebirds

Eastern bluebird

Western bluebird

Mountain bluebird

Bluebirds are real crowd-pleasers. North America boasts three distinct species: eastern bluebirds in the east and both western and mountain bluebirds in the west.

Many, many years ago, the return of bluebirds—especially the eastern bluebird—to northern states in March signaled the arrival of warm weather. But with mild winters becoming more common, many bluebirds now spend winters in their nesting areas all across the North.

Making a Comeback

In the early to mid-1900s, bluebirds were almost declared extinct. But today, happily, all three bluebird species—mountain, eastern and western—are at healthy population levels, and their future looks bright.

They still face challenges, however, such as competition for nesting sites from house sparrows, house wrens, tree swallows and European starlings. Often, just about the time a pair of bluebirds is ready to settle into a nest, one of these bully birds takes over.

Food of Choice

If you want to feed them in your own backyard, provide mealworms. Live worms are always best, but you can try dried mealworms as well. If you're feeling ambitious, raise your own mealworms for an unending supply.

Backyard Favorites

If you've had some trouble attracting bluebirds in the past, follow these four steps. First, get a nest box especially designed for them. Second, hang it so it faces an open area or field. Third, offer mealworms. Fourth and finally, don't forget the birdbath, which is a big hit with bluebirds. And here's one more bonus suggestion—plant native trees and shrubs that have berries. Bluebirds will stick around all year, and they need something to eat in fall and winter!

Nesting Habits

To the accompaniment of his own incessant warbling, the male pursues his chosen mate from one perch to another, often showing her spots available for nesting.

Nesting starts early among bluebirds, so they can raise at least two broods each year. It's common for the first brood to help their parents feed the second brood, a practice known as "cooperative breeding." As the old song says, this popular and lovely bird truly is the "bluebird of happiness," bringing excitement, color and adventure to any backyard.

Many will raise one to three broods per season. Females lay two to seven pale blue (occasionally white) eggs, and once the young hatch, they fledge about three weeks later.

Fascinating Facts

Bluebirds can only be found in the backyards and farmland of North America. You can't find another group quite like them anywhere else in the world.

 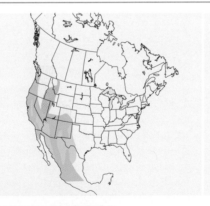 

EASTERN, WESTERN AND MOUNTAIN BLUEBIRD

SIALIA SIALIS, S. MEXICANA and *S. CURRUCOIDES,* respectively.

Length: 7 inches.

Wingspan: 13 to 14 inches.

Distinctive Markings: Males generally have a blue back, wings and head, with a white belly, except for the mountain bluebird, which is brilliant blue all over. Orange on the breast extends onto the throat on eastern bluebirds. Females generally have the same markings, but duller, except for western females, which are grayish with pretty pale blue feathers on the tail and wings.

Voice: Soft *tru-al-ly, tru-al-ly* warble for eastern; mountain is similar but higher pitched; and western's is a subdued *f-few, f-few, f-few.*

Habitat: Backyards and farmland.

Nesting: Built mostly by the female, the nest is made of dried grasses and lined with finer grasses, hair and feathers. She lays two to seven pale blue eggs between the months of March and July for eastern, April and May for western, and between April and July for mountain bluebirds.

Diet: Insects and berries.

Backyard Favorite:
Live mealworms.

Cardinals

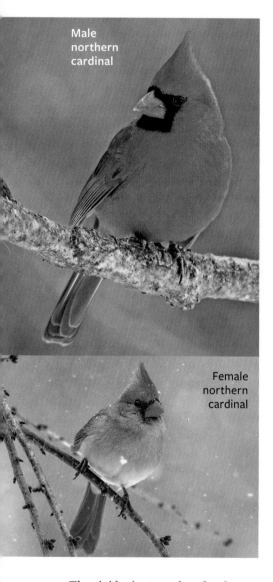

Male northern cardinal

Female northern cardinal

The vivid crimson color of male cardinals comes from carotenoid pigments, which are found in red fruits. Eating more of these vibrant scarlet-hued snacks, especially during molt, helps a male form brighter red feathers. The flashy color boosts his ability to successfully attract mates and defend a pair's nesting territory.

Setting out a bird feeder with black oil sunflower seeds is a surefire way to attract northern cardinals—but gardeners shouldn't stop there, because the right plants bring in these beauties. The key is the trifecta of providing food, cover and places to raise young, says Gary Ritchison, an ornithologist at Eastern Kentucky University and author of *Northern Cardinal*.

A Bill Built for Seed

The downward curve of cardinals' bills, typical of most seed-eating birds, allows them to open or crush tough seeds. They also have larger jaw muscles than many other songbirds, which means they can consume bigger seeds. When selecting plants, look for some with medium-sized seeds as well as a mixture of seasonality.

Many gardeners have luck with Purple Majesty millet, nasturtium, purple coneflower, safflower, corn, sunflower and sweet pea.

Year-Round Residents

Cardinals also eat wild fruits. As nonmigratory birds, they seek a variety of foods as availability changes through the year. "They're pretty adaptive," Gary says. "They have to be, as a resident bird."

But as they consume fruits, studies suggest, cardinals still are after the seeds, often discarding much of the fruit pulp. For that reason, try fruits with larger seeds.

They're drawn to berry plants like dogwood, hackberry, northern bayberry and serviceberry.

Host a Pair

For cardinal nests, concealment is key: They look for the camouflage of dense shrubs and small trees. Their nests are low, only 4 to 8 feet off the ground. Breeding males stay near the nest, so try bringing in a nesting pair to see them year-round.

For their first nests in April or May, they often choose dense evergreens. Pairs raise several broods a year and will select different sites. Wild grape is a nice addition to a yard because the birds use its bark for nesting material.

Cardinals hide in box elder, rose, eastern red cedar, hawthorn, wild grape and nannyberry.

NORTHERN CARDINAL
CARDINALIS CARDINALIS

Length: 8¾ inches.

Wingspan: 12 inches.

Distinctive Markings: Male is bright red with a black face. Also has a prominent crest and red bill. Female is fawn colored with red accents.

Voice: Over two dozen different songs. The most common song is: *What cheer! What cheer! What cheer!*

Habitat: Sheltered backyards, woodland edges and parks.

Nesting: Three or four whitish gray eggs with brown speckles. Builds a nest of twigs and grasses hidden in dense trees or shrubs.

Diet: Seeds in winter; insects, such as beetles and cicadas, in the summer; berries and other fruits when they are available and in season.

Backyard Favorites: Sunflower seeds, safflower seeds and cracked corn.

Chickadees

Black-capped chickadee

There are seven species of chickadees in North America, but depending on where you live, you'll probably see only one or two of these four: Carolina, black-capped, mountain and boreal. The black-capped is considered a classic backyard favorite and is found at feeders throughout much of the continent.

Listen for the Call

Whichever kind of species you find, all are about 5 inches tall and have snazzy dark caps and black bibs. The call is a version of their own name and varies in pitch, speed and clarity depending on the species. The easiest version to learn to recognize is that of the black-capped chickadee with its *chick-a-dee-dee-dee* call.

Chickadees are talkative, with a whole repertoire of high, wheezy notes in addition to the trademark call. In spring, black-cappeds sing a loud two- to three-note *fee-bee* mating call. A super high-pitched *seeee* is a warning that there is

a predator around, and every chickadee within hearing distance freezes upon hearing it. That watchfulness may contribute to the bird's surprisingly long life span—about 10 years!

On the Move

Chickadees are always on the move, picking off insects at any stage of their life cycle—from eggs and larvae to pupae and adults—from leaves and branches. Pairs remain together year-round, and from fall through early spring, chickadees form small roaming flocks with groups of titmice, nuthatches and warblers.

Little Bird, Big Family

All chickadee species can be seen within their respective range throughout the year, although they visit backyard feeders less often in spring and summer, when insects are at their peak. However, chickadees lay as many as 10 eggs per year, and that's a lot of mouths to feed. If a chickadee has a hungry spring brood, it will most likely become a regular at a seed feeder.

Sunflower Seed Fans

Chickadees aren't a picky bunch, which makes it even easier to bring them into your yard. After all, you don't have to buy expensive, fancy seed mixes—black oil sunflower seed is all it often takes. They'll also come in for Nyjer, suet, peanuts and striped sunflower seed.

Garden Picks

Chickadees also love berries, so plant berry-producing trees and shrubs in your garden to bring in more winter visitors. Viburnum is a good start. And for summer

birds, don't forget to plant sunflowers. They'll pick the sunflower seeds right from the heads once dry.

A Bird in the Hand

Keep those birdbaths fresh and full. If you do, you might even see several chickadees gather at once. And try to feed them from your hand; they really are one of the easiest birds to do this with. To give it a whirl, remove your usual feeders and just offer seed in your hand. Dress warmly, stay as still as possible and be patient.

BLACK-CAPPED CHICKADEE
POECILE ATRICAPILLUS

Length: 5¼ inches.

Wingspan: 8 inches.

Distinctive Markings: Black cap and chin, white cheeks and gray back.

Voice: *Chick-a-dee-dee-dee* is its call, which many will recognize. Its song is a *fee-bee* tune.

Habitat: Woodlands, thickets, parks and wooded yards.

Nesting: Six to eight white eggs with brown spots. Uses birdhouses and natural cavities to protect its nest made of plant fibers, wool, hair and pieces of moss.

Diet: Insects, berries and seeds.

Backyard Favorites: Sunflower seeds, suet and Nyjer.

Finches

Adult male purple finch, top

Two birds, the house and the purple finch: Both common visitors in the backyard, they can be particularly tricky to tell apart. The purple finch is chunkier, shorter-tailed and redder overall than the house finch, while the adult male house finch sports a rosy head and underside, with grayish streaks on the back and darker stripes on the sides. Females and juvenile house finches are much drabber, resembling sparrows.

A Wide Range

The house finch is commonly found throughout much of the Lower 48, while the range of the purple finch is restricted to the dense forests of the West Coast, southern Canada and the northeastern U.S. during breeding season. And purple finches may be seen anywhere in the southeastern states during fall, winter and spring.

Before its expansion throughout the U.S., the house finch was native to the Southwest and was acclimated to an open, arid habitat. "You see them so often in our developed human-dominated landscapes because we've created open areas similar to their native habitat," says Trina Bayard, bird conservation director at Audubon Washington.

House finch

DID YOU KNOW?
House finches travel in flocks, sometimes with 50 or more birds. They are extremely social and are rarely seen alone.

Color Change-Up

The difference between these birds becomes clear when you compare the adult males. Purple finches are a deep cranberry or raspberry color on most of their body. Male house finches are more orange and red with the color concentrated on their heads and chests. Females are more difficult to tell apart, so look closely at their faces: Purple finches have a bolder face pattern, with two white stripes stretching from their beaks to the nape of their necks.

Nesting Habits

The nesting habits of the two birds are completely different. House finches nest on the edges of open areas, sometimes on street lamps or in ivy on the sides of buildings. Purple finches nest primarily in forest conifers or dense shrubs, and at times in landscaped areas with trees. Neither species uses birdhouses.

Bird Behavior

"Seemingly similar birds can be really different from each other," Trina says. "The house finch is a very social bird," which nests in colonies or groups. Purple finches often nest on their own. In the winter, however, they're happy to join flocks with pine siskins and goldfinches.

Food Favorites

Both species enjoy sunflower seeds in the winter. During summer, they eat fruits, berries and seeds from native plants, along with bugs.

Plant flowers that will produce good seed at the end of summer. You can offer some annuals like sunflowers and cosmos, but you'll also want to invest in easy-to-grow perennials such as black-eyed Susans, coneflowers, purple millet and Shasta daisies.

Both species are drawn to feeders, and Trina suggests filling them with unhulled black oil sunflower seeds.

House finches are among the few birds that prefer to feed their young this kind of food, rather than insects or worms. You'll see them at your sunflower, thistle and fruit feeders. No wonder they like backyards!

HOUSE FINCH
CARPODACUS MEXICANUS

Length: 6 inches.
Wingspan: 9½ inches.
Distinctive Markings: Males have reddish foreheads, breasts and rumps. Females and juveniles are streaked grayish brown. All have brown-streaked bellies.
Voice: A varied warble, often ending in a long *veeerrr*.
Habitat: Any wooded area or backyard.
Nesting: Low in shrubs, door wreaths or hanging baskets; lays four to five spotted bluish white eggs.
Diet: Seeds of berries and weeds.
Backyard Favorites: Sunflower, Nyjer, mixed birdseed, peanuts, fruit, suet and sugar water.

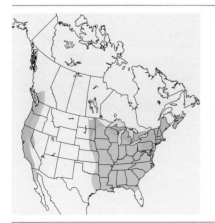

PURPLE FINCH
CARPODACUS PURPUREUS

Length: 6 inches.
Wingspan: 10 inches.
Distinctive Markings: Male has a raspberry tinge, brightest on head and rump. Tail is notched. The females and juveniles are brown-gray striped.
Voice: A *fridi ferdi frididifri fridi frr* call.

Habitat: Swamps, along streams and hillsides.
Nesting: Prefers trees in dense foliage. Female lays four to five speckled pale green-blue eggs.
Diet: Mostly a seed eater, but also eats weeds, grasses, berries, beetles and caterpillars.
Backyard Favorites: Sunflower seeds and millet.

Male
American
goldfinch

GROW A GOLDFINCH GARDEN

They'll seek out the seeds of plants in the massive *Asteraceae* (*Compositae*) family, including sunflower, black-eyed Susan, purple coneflower and aster. They also gravitate toward grasses and weedy plants.

Goldfinches

American goldfinches are some of the most common feeder birds across the country. They are beloved year-round residents in most of North America and will reach Canada in summer and the lower part of the United States in winter.

Males vs. Females

Males have bright, sunny plumage on their back, breast and belly in spring and summer, with a distinct solid black cap on top of their heads and black wings with white wing marks. Females are slightly duller and lack the cap. They both have a pinkish cone-shaped bill to crack open seeds like sunflower and thistle, and feet with three toes in front and one in back for perching on small branches and stems.

Wardrobe Change

In fall, the male's vibrancy fades as plain brown feathers grow in, and they transform to look more like females. The full molting process may take six to eight weeks, and during that time goldfinches appear patchy. In fall, both start to fade in color to a pale yellow or olive-gray shade. Many people think goldfinches disappear after summer, but they're still there—sporting a different look.

Food of Choice

Goldfinches love thistle seed, also known as Nyjer. You can pick up a simple mesh bag thistle feeder for a few bucks to see if you can attract goldfinches, or invest a little extra to get a nice tube feeder. If you do, you'll have happy goldfinches for years.

Nesting Habits

Goldfinches are among the latest nesters in North America. They wait for the flowers to produce fibrous seeds so they can use them to build their nests, along with rootlets and spider silk. Males and females find the nesting site together. Then the females build their nests in about six days, and lay two to seven pale bluish eggs.

Fascinating Facts

You won't find American goldfinches eating insects or worms. They survive almost exclusively on seeds, which makes them a relative rarity among songbirds. They start their young on a seed diet early as well.

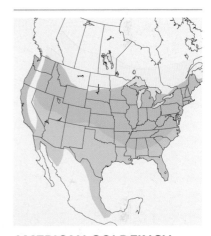

AMERICAN GOLDFINCH
CARDUELIS TRISTIS

Length: 4½ to 5½ inches.

Wingspan: 9 inches.

Distinctive Markings: In spring and summer, males are bright yellow with black wings, tail and forehead. Females are a duller yellow with white wing bars. In winter, both are olive-brown with wing bars.

Voice: Melodic flight call, *per-chick-o-ree, per-chick-o-ree.* Courtship song is a canarylike sweet song.

Habitat: Open areas such as yards, fields and groves.

Nesting: Cup-shaped nest with up to seven pale blue eggs.

Diet: Seeds and berries.

Backyard Favorite: Supply Nyjer in a tube feeder with multiple ports, or in a nylon stocking.

Female American goldfinch

Male
ruby-throated
hummingbird

DID YOU KNOW?

Hummingbirds love red. So be sure to plant enough red flowers to keep them coming back for more. Choose a combo that blooms from spring through fall so that flowers are still blooming when fall migration begins.

Hummingbirds

Hummingbirds seem to exist in a different dimension from other birds. The fact that you can witness the magic show in your gardens—or right outside your windows—makes them more endearing. These little acrobatic fliers are captivating creatures adored by backyard birders. It's easy to see why. Their charm and antics elicit huge smiles and enthusiastic *oohs* and *aahs* from onlookers like no other bird does! These mini marvels zip, zoom and fly forward, backward, sideways, up and down. They even hover in midair at flowers and feeders. Their wings move in a figure-eight pattern, which allows them to fly through the air with ease.

Hummers go where the food is, and to colors they love the most: red, orange and rich pink. That's why planting nectar-filled plants with blooms in these hues is a great way to bring them in. The same goes for sugar-water feeders. Keep in mind, however, that hummingbirds are very territorial and fiercely protect their food sources, so consider putting out more than one feeder!

Ruby-throated hummingbirds are probably the species backyard birders know best, as they are the only ones that nest in the entire eastern half of the United States and part of Canada.

Endless Energy

The hummingbirds' miniature dimensions make them all the more amazing. A ruby-throat or rufous weighs about one-ninth of an ounce. That's lighter than a nickel!

The sight of a hummer darting about a garden is even more impressive when we break this high-speed action down by the numbers. A hummingbird at rest may breathe four times per second, and its heart may beat more than 20 times per second.

A hummingbird may also beat its wings 80 times a second. To get a sense of what this means, stand and flap your arms as fast as you can for a few moments. If you concentrate, you should be able to flap four times in a second. Now imagine doing this same action a whopping 20 times faster—an impossible feat for a human, but nothing remarkable for a tiny hummingbird.

At first glance, hummingbirds often seem delightfully tame, even confiding. Sometimes they'll come astonishingly close, especially when you're near a feeder or other tempting nectar source.

Think about it from their view, though. Humans must seem like incredibly big, slow creatures to them. Hummingbirds are likely to be more interested in things closer to their own size and speed.

If you love hummingbirds, you have to appreciate spiders. Hummers often use bits of spiderweb for their nests. Strong, lightweight and super sticky, it's

Female
ruby-throated
hummingbird

RUBY-THROATED HUMMINGBIRD
ARCHILOCHUS COLUBRIS

Length: 3¾ inches.
Wingspan: 4½ inches.
Distinctive Markings: Ruby-red throat on male; both sexes have a showy metallic-green back and head.
Voice: Faint; a very rapid series of chipping notes.
Habitat: Areas with plenty of colorful, nectar-rich flowers.

Nesting: Builds a cup-shaped nest the diameter of a quarter and camouflaged with lichens. Lays two tiny white eggs.
Diet: Nectar, insects and tree sap.
Backyard Favorites: Sugar water and bright, trumpet-shaped flowers.

Anna's
hummingbird

a perfect nest material, allowing for compact nests that will stretch and grow as baby hummers get bigger.

Protecting Their Turf

An endless sugar rush fuels all the high-speed comings and goings of these miniature marvels. Many birds feed on nectar, but none do it as consistently as hummingbirds. And this dependence on flower nectar drives much of their interesting and acrobatic behavior.

Consider their defense of territory. Hummingbirds may defend their temporary feeding territory at any time of the year. Flowers can produce only so much nectar in a day, so if a hummer finds a good patch of blooms, it may start defending that specific patch, driving away other hummers.

All the zooming and chattering of hummingbirds chasing away

rivals may seem like a waste of energy to us, but it may be easier than flying off and finding another flower patch. It becomes somewhat comical, though, when the instinct carries over to hummingbirds visiting feeders. The feeders may have a vast supply of sugar water, but the birds don't see it that way. The instinct to guard their food source is so strong that they continue to chase off rival birds.

The reliance on flowers also drives their migration patterns. In the West, for example, species like the rufous, broad-tailed and Calliope migrate north through the deserts and valleys in very early spring, and south through the mountain meadows in late summer. Why? Because that's where the flowers are. In early spring the mountain meadows are still covered with snow, while in late summer the valleys may be hot and dry, so hummers have adapted their routes to follow the blooming seasons.

Garden for Hummingbirds

If you want to create the perfect hummingbird garden, you'll find books and websites dedicated to the subject, so consult some resources and start working on a space today.

Don't have the space to start a whole new garden? Containers are a solution with style. Hanging baskets add flair and can offer a good home to nectar-producing plants.

Consider planting native plants, which almost always suit the needs of local hummers. Planting native plants, vines, shrubs and trees suited to your growing conditions will feed and shelter hummingbirds for many years to come. Bee balm, phlox and salvia are just a few of the native perennials to choose that hummingbirds can't resist.

Put Out a Buffet

In addition to offering nectar-rich plants for hummers, it's a good idea to put out sugar water. Simply combine 4 parts hot water to 1 part sugar. Mix it up until it's completely dissolved. Once it cools to room temperature, it's ready. Of course, the hummingbirds in your area will do just fine without it, but if you want an up-close view, this is the way to get it. Put out several sugar-water feeders far enough apart that hummers can't see one another (to accommodate their territorial nature).

Invite insects, too. Small ones, which they catch in the air or on the leaves of plants, provide the protein hummingbirds need to maintain

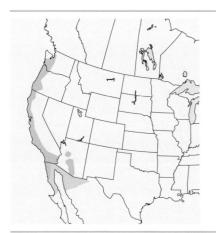

ANNA'S HUMMINGBIRD
CALYPTE ANNA

Length: 4 inches.
Wingspan: 5¼ inches.
Distinctive Markings: Adult males have an iridescent red crown and throat. Females have a red patch on the throat and white markings over eyes.
Voice: Call is a high sharp *stit*.

Habitat: Lush gardens and parks that provide nectar-producing flowers.
Nesting: Made of plant down held together with spider webs. Females lay two small white eggs.
Diet: Nectar, sugar water, spiders, small insects and tree sap.
Backyard Favorite: Sugar water.

their busy bodies and grow new feathers. Eliminate insecticides to keep the insect population thriving.

Offer Plenty of Water

Along with food and shelter, water is one of the three necessities of every backyard habitat. A larger water feature is a great addition and will attract a variety of birds, but consider adding a shallow birdbath or mister. Hummingbirds flock to most water sources, especially in summer's heat. They love any type of moving water.

Reduce chemical use. When you have hummingbirds exploring your backyard, the last thing you want is for them to be harmed by pesticides or herbicides. Make an effort to reduce chemical use for the health of wildlife.

Create a Safe Space

Be sure to provide protective cover from predators and the weather by planting shrubbery, especially around the perimeter of your yard. Doing so also encourages hummingbirds to take up residence in your backyard, giving you the chance to see them.

Keep cats inside. It may be hard for some. But roaming cats are a leading cause of bird deaths, so it's best if they stay inside.

Also, never underestimate the value of a good tree. If you plan it right, a good tree can offer many benefits to hummingbirds, including nectar in spring and nesting space in summer. Go ahead and invest in a new tree for your backyard. We promise you won't be sorry.

BLACK-CHINNED HUMMINGBIRD
ARCHILOCHUS ALEXANDRI

Length: 3¾ inches.

Wingspan: 4¾ inches.

Distinctive Markings: Male has a black chin with a purple band below it. Female's throat is pale.

Voice: A high, weak warble.

Habitat: Mountainous areas from foothills to summits, gardens and areas near rivers.

Nesting: A round cup made of plant down, about 1½ inches across and coated with spider silk, usually attached to a branch or tree fork. Females lay two white eggs.

Diet: Flower nectar, tree sap, pollen and insects.

Backyard Favorite: Sugar water.

Rufous hummingbird

Black-chinned hummingbird

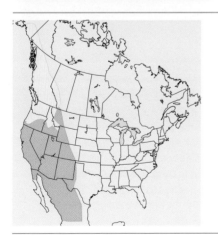

RUFOUS HUMMINGBIRD
SELASPHORUS RUFUS

Length: 3¾ inches.

Wingspan: 4½ inches.

Distinctive Markings: Male is reddish brown on back, head and tail; scarlet throat. Female is metallic green above, with pale, rust-colored sides.

Voice: Call note is *chewp chewp*.

Habitat: Open areas and along woodland edges.

Nesting: May nest in loose colonies, with up to 10 nests.

Diet: Nectar and tree sap.

Backyard Favorites: Attracted to red flowers; sugar water at feeders.

Jays

Blue jay

Jays are the loudest and flashiest of the Corvidae family, which also includes crows, ravens and magpies. They're also considered to be among the most intelligent species of the bird world. Most jays have strong bills and feed on all sorts of food, but these birds especially love peanuts. Although at least 10 species live in North America, this spotlight is on the three most likely to visit your backyard. Whether you think they're brilliant, bullies or both, there's plenty to discover about these clever corvids.

Blue Jay

Blue jays are some of the biggest, brassiest and most colorful backyard birds in North America. Though some people find them too bold and loud, many more welcome any sighting of this beautiful flier. Although a rare visitor west of the Rocky Mountains, it lives throughout the Midwest and East, and it's hard to miss thanks to its bright blue markings and loud *jayyy jayyy* call.

At 11 to 12 inches and sporting bright blue feathers, jays are a sight when they pass through your yard. Males and females are difficult to tell apart, so you might want to refrain from calling the blue jay hanging out in your tree a "he." The species is distinguished by a prominent crest and noticeable white and black patterns through the predominant blue.

This bird doesn't need much coaxing to visit backyards and will stop by most seed or suet feeders, but plenty of peanuts, acorns and beechnuts may be the ticket when it comes to attracting a yard full of jays. Some people see these birds as bullies. To discourage their visits, hang feeders with foods jays don't eat, like Nyjer, and use perchless feeders designed for smaller birds.

Blue jay parents take part in nest building, with males usually doing more of the gathering and females specializing in the construction, typically in the crook of a tree. It's not uncommon for jays to start building more than one nest; if they detect a predator, they'll move right away. Females lay up to seven eggs. Once they hatch, young fledge at between two and three weeks old.

Steller's Jay

The next time you hear a quick *shek-shek-shek* in the mountainous West, look up, and you might spot a Steller's jay. Common in evergreen

BLUE JAY
CYANOCITTA CRISTATA

Length: 11 inches.
Wingspan: 16 inches.
Distinctive Markings: Blue feathers and crest with a gray breast.
Voice: Harsh scream: *jaaay, jaaay, jaaay.*
Habitat: Backyards, parks and woodlands.

Nesting: Well hidden and often found in the crotch of a tree 10 to 25 feet above the ground. Builds a false nest of twigs before actual nest; lays up to seven brown-spotted greenish eggs.
Diet: Nuts, seeds, fruits, insects and even frogs.
Backyard Favorites: Suet, sunflower seeds and peanuts.

forests, the species typically sticks to exploring the higher canopies but will swoop into backyards to stop by feeders. It's the only all-dark jay with a crest, and it has small white or blue spots on its forehead. These birds travel in flocks except when nesting, and they eat loads of seeds, berries and insects. They are known to nibble on unattended picnic lunches, too!

Western Scrub-Jay

This crestless species is found in—you guessed it—the U.S. West. Western scrub-jays are common in parks and woodlands across coastal California, but the species also lives inland, where it presents with paler, grayer markings. Like their cousins, they're omnivorous, meaning they eat both insects and plant material. They typically bury their favorite food, acorns, for later. To identify, look for a white throat and a gray back. Westerns go off on their own to breed in isolated pairs instead of staying within a large flock as Florida scrub-jays do. Nests, built by both parents, are cup-shaped and made of twigs and moss.

Backyard Favorites

You can't go wrong with peanuts, either in or out of the shell, for jays. Some put them out on a tray feeder, though this makes easy pickings for squirrels. You can invest in a peanut feeder. Jays also love acorns; gather some in fall to offer at your feeder.

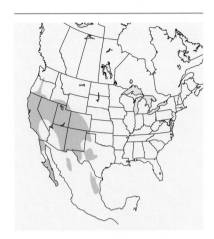

WESTERN SCRUB-JAY
APHELOCOMA CALIFORNICA

Length: 11½ inches.
Wingspan: 15½ inches.
Distinctive Markings: Bright blue with a white belly and gray patch on back. Sexes look alike.
Voice: Hoarse rising call of *shreeeenk* or a rapid series *quay-quay-quay* or *cheek-cheek-cheek*.
Habitat: Dense shrubbery in wooded parks and backyards.
Nesting: Bulky nest of twigs in a low tree or shrub.
Diet: Nuts, fruits, insects and even small animals.
Backyard Favorites: Peanuts, suet, sunflower seeds and cracked corn.

Steller's jay

Western scrub-jay

STELLER'S JAY
CYANOCITTA STELLERI

Length: 11½ inches.
Wingspan: 19 inches.
Distinctive Markings: Crest and front part of body are a sooty black. The rest of body is cobalt blue or purplish.
Voice: A harsh *shaaaaar* or rapid *shek shek shek shek*.
Habitat: Evergreen forests, open areas and mountains.

Nesting: Bulky nest of large sticks held together with mud. Usually built in the fork of an evergreen.
Diet: Forages for acorns, pine seeds, fruit, insects, frogs and young of smaller birds.
Backyard Favorites: Sunflower seed and peanuts.

DID YOU KNOW?

Juncos are part of the sparrow family. Look for these dark-eyed beauties in flocks with sparrows and bluebirds.

Dark-eyed junco

Juncos

Dark-eyed juncos reappear in many parts of the Lower 48 just as winter comes alive each year. They leave their breeding grounds in the North Woods and the western mountains to descend on backyard feeding stations across much of the U.S. Many people, like *Birds & Blooms* reader Jennifer Hardison from Athens, Tennessee, have a nickname for juncos. "We call them snowbirds because we only see them after a snowfall," she says.

Juncos are thriving. According to bird experts at the Cornell Lab of Ornithology, their total population is estimated to be more than a whopping 630 million!

To attract a flock of these backyard favorites, all it takes are a couple of feeders and the right plants to bring them in.

Serve the Right Stuff

In winter, juncos feast on seeds of weeds and grasses that are left in your landscape or in fields, parks and open woodlands. Seeds from common plants such as chickweed, buckwheat, lamb's quarters and sorrel make up 75% of their year-round diet. But juncos also supplement with feeder foods. These snowbirds prefer to forage on the ground for millet, black oil sunflower seed, sunflower hearts or cracked corn that has fallen from feeders. Occasionally they may steal a seed from a platform or a tray feeder, too, or snatch a juicy berry from a fruit-producing backyard shrub.

Nesting Habits

Although juncos nest mostly in Canada and parts of Alaska, there are some year-round residents in pockets in the contiguous U.S., including the Northwest and the California coast. They are ground nesters and lay three to six eggs with each brood.

East vs. West

Depending on where you live, your juncos may look different. Those found in the eastern half of the U.S. are charcoal gray on top with white bellies and known as slate-colored types. The most common variety in the west is called the Oregon junco. Male Oregons sport a solid black or slaty hood, chestnut-colored back, rusty sides and a white belly. Other juncos, like the white-winged and gray-headed, are less common and have limited ranges. Where junco ranges overlap, though, you may find several types in one winter flock. And when you locate them, look for their signature detail—a pretty pink bill.

DARK-EYED JUNCO
JUNCO HYEMALIS

Length: 6¼ inches.

Wingspan: 9¼ inches.

Distinctive Markings: Common characteristics are dark eyes, white-edged tails and dark-hooded heads; juncos interbreed with each other freely.

Voice: Trills vary, from dry notes to tingling sounds.

Habitat: Near feeders, forests and in bogs.

Nesting: Cup-shaped nest on ground. Lays three to six eggs.

Diet: Seeds, nuts and grains in winter; insects, berries and grass seeds in summer.

Backyard Favorites: Birdseed and cracked corn on the ground.

Slate-colored junco

Oregon junco

FROM LEFT: JOHN GILL; MARIE READ (2)

Red-breasted
nuthatch

White-breasted
nuthatch

USING THEIR HEADS

Whenever you see a bird going
headfirst down a tree trunk, it's
probably a nuthatch. Extremely
fun to watch, they are among the
most acrobatic bird species.

Nuthatches

Nuthatches are favorite backyard visitors because they are energetic little birds that never fail to entertain. Both red-breasted and white-breasted nuthatches are common throughout the United States. You'll see them circling tree trunks, moving up, down and around as they probe the bark for their next meal.

Food of Choice

Insects are the main food source for nuthatches. The birds search bark and crevices for treats like beetles, spiders, ants and caterpillars as they dance around tree trunks.

Backyard Favorites

Nuthatches are happy to visit your backyard feeder, especially if you have a yard full of trees they can use for foraging and shelter. Stock your feeders with black oil sunflower seeds. Because bully birds also seek out black oil seeds, a tube feeder with small perches is best.

If you don't have a peanut feeder yet, get your hands on one for this upcoming cold season. Both red and white-breasted nuthatches will surely entertain you for hours as they scurry up, down and around a peanut feeder. Their favorite? Out of the shell, unsalted peanuts.

Set a Mealworm Menu

More species than just bluebirds enjoy a mealworm snack. A large portion of the nuthatch diet is insects, so putting out mealworms for them is definitely worth a shot. They don't require anything fancy; just toss some mealworms in a shallow tray or platform feeder.

Don't Forget Suet

Whether you make your own or buy it, a suet block in a cagelike feeder is sure to lure in nuthatches. In the winter months, when conifer seeds are sometimes scarce, hungry red-breasted nuthatches will travel in search of food and will likely stop at feeders for a suet snack. Add peanut butter to your DIY suet mixture and white-breasted nuthatches will love it even more!

Nesting Habits

White-breasted nuthatches may sometimes use nest boxes, so you may get lucky and have a nesting pair. Although they're small birds, they don't seem to mind nesting in larger cavities or abandoned woodpecker holes. Unfortunately, red-breasted nuthatches rarely use nest boxes. Look for their nests in existing holes in aspen trees.

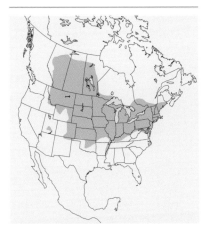

WHITE-BREASTED NUTHATCH
SITTA CAROLINENSIS

Length: 5¾ inches.

Wingspan: 11 inches.

Distinctive Markings: Males and females look similar, with a blue-gray back and wings, black cap and bright white breast.

Voice: Nasal *yank-yank-yank* call.

Habitat: Areas with plentiful trees.

Nesting: Builds in natural cavities and birdhouses. Lays about five to 10 white eggs with multicolored markings on them.

Diet: Insects and larvae; tree nuts, seeds and berries.

Backyard Favorites: Sunflower seeds, unsalted peanuts, birdseed mix and suet.

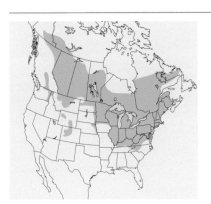

RED-BREASTED NUTHATCH
SITTA CANADENSIS

Length: 4½ inches.

Wingspan: 8½ inches.

Distinctive Markings: Black eye line with a white stripe directly above it, rust-colored breast; female is similar.

Voice: A high-pitched nasal *yenk, yenk, yenk*.

Habitat: Evergreen forests, and wooded yards and parks.

Nesting: Hole or cavity in a tree or a nest box.

Diet: Insects, berries, nuts and seeds.

Backyard Favorites: Sunflower seeds and suet.

DID YOU KNOW?

When not at feeders, Baltimore orioles feed on insects high in trees. Their rich, varied whistles and chattering calls are often heard before they're spotted in the canopies.

Baltimore oriole

Orioles

Few songbirds are more visually striking—or create more excitement for birders—than orioles.

"Oriole" is based on several Latin words that all mean "golden." The name was first applied to a European bird, a member of what is now called the Old World oriole family. However, American orioles are completely unrelated. American orioles are classified in the blackbird family, along with such birds as grackles, red-winged blackbirds and meadowlarks. Unlike other members, however, they spend most of their time high up in the treetops, rather than on the ground.

The Backyard Stars

Nine different kinds of orioles live throughout the continental U.S. during breeding months, but the most common are the Baltimore, Bullock's, orchard, hooded and Scott's. The other four—altimera, Audubon's, spot-breasted and streak-backed—are rarely spotted or they occupy very small territories along the country's southern borders.

The Baltimore oriole, common all around the East in the warmer months, is the most well-known member of the clan.

Male Baltimore and Bullock's orioles add dazzling color to many backyards in summer—Baltimores in the East, Bullock's in the West. Where they meet on the western Great Plains, the two sometimes interbreed, creating hybrids. For a few years they were categorized into one species called "northern oriole," and you can still find that name in some older books.

Most fly to the tropics for the winter, but increasing numbers of Baltimore orioles are now staying through the cold months in some eastern states where people keep feeders filled to attract them.

About 8 inches long, with a 9- to 12-inch wingspan, Baltimores are medium-sized songbirds. Like all other blackbirds, they have a thick, pointed bill. The vibrant underparts, shoulders and rump of the males can vary from orange to yellow-orange. Mature females and juveniles tend to be more dull, with yellow-brown feathers and dark barred wings.

Widespread in the East and parts of the Southwest in summer, orchard orioles are smaller than other orioles, and adult males have a unique color combination with deep chestnut instead of orange and yellow.

The Southwest Duo: Hooded and Scott's

In summer, hooded orioles are common from coastal California to southern Texas, chiefly in lowland riversides, canyons and backyards. They often place their nests in palm trees, using the long, strong fibers of palm leaves as nesting material. But if no palms are available, they'll readily nest in sycamores, cottonwoods or other trees. Adult males are primarily orange (including an orange "hood") with black accents.

Scott's orioles are found from eastern California and northern Utah to the Hill Country of central Texas. Open woodlands of juniper or oak may be good habitats for them, but they're especially drawn

Bullock's oriole

Orchard oriole

Hooded oriole

to areas with lots of yucca plants, building their nests among the long, daggerlike yucca leaves. The rich, bubbling song of the male Scott's oriole carries for long distances across arid hillsides.

Nesting Habits

These flamboyant birds spend winters from the southeastern states through Central America and northern South America. They migrate north to breed from Georgia to southern Canada. When orioles return to their northern breeding territories, they look for tree cover and stay well hidden in their search for food. During the spring mating season, males attract females by singing, chattering and hopping from branch to branch. If a female is interested, the male bows and fans his wings and tail, then the female responds by singing and quivering her wings.

The females do most of the work of building the nest. Woven from fibers of grasses, grapevines and milkweed, their nests are marvels of avian architecture: hanging

pouches or bags, attached by their edges and suspended from twigs. Many oriole nests are deeper than they are wide, and despite their distinctive appearance, they can be hard to spot, because they're often surrounded by heavy foliage. Backyard birders often discover an oriole nest in their trees only after the leaves have fallen in autumn. Elms, cottonwoods, maples, willows and apple trees are among the sites favored for nesting.

The female lays three to six pale gray-blue eggs, which take two weeks to hatch. Both parents care for the chicks, with males chipping in with the feeding of the young, which fledge two weeks later.

If there's no threat of raptors or cats, a mother oriole may bring her fledglings to a backyard feeder. Be sure to listen each spring for their loud, rich, melodic song in a tree above you, as if they're whistling a tune to tell you where to find them.

Bring Them In

No matter what the species is, if you cover the basics—trees, fruit and sugar water—there's a good chance a flashy oriole will pay a visit to your backyard, no matter where you live in the continental United States, in spring.

Orioles love trees, especially many native varieties. Top choices will depend on where you live, but along with elms and cottonwoods,

Baltimore oriole enjoying an orange

sycamores are typically a good option. Orioles also prefer the native trees and shrubs that bear dark-colored fruit.

More than most songbirds, orioles love nectar, and they may visit some of the same tubular red flowers that attract hummingbirds.

Orioles will come to feeders that contain a mix of one part sugar and four parts water—no artificial coloring needed! They will come to regular hummingbird feeders if they have large enough perches, or you can buy orange-colored feeders designed for orioles.

Orioles absolutely love fresh fruit. Red cherries and red grapes attract them (not yellow cherries or green grapes), but they especially adore oranges! Half of an orange, impaled on a stick, makes an easy and irresistible snack. Baltimores

Scott's oriole

use a technique called gaping to get juice out of fruit. They stab a ripe berry or orange with a closed bill, then open wide and lap up the droplets with their tongues.

Even a small dish of grape jelly may attract orioles, catbirds and other popular backyard fliers.

Orioles also like to dine on insects, which they sometimes catch in the air. They'll also hang upside down or perform other

athletic moves to catch bugs or caterpillars. These flashy fliers dine on furry caterpillars that other birds won't touch. They whack them on a branch to remove the hair, and then they gulp them down.

And try putting out a deep dish of live or dried mealworms: you might just draw a hungry crowd of golden birds.

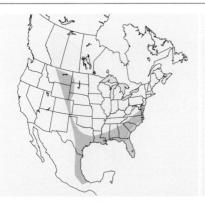

BALTIMORE, BULLOCK'S AND ORCHARD ORIOLE

ICTERUS GALBUBA, I. BULLOCKII AND *I. SPURIOUS*, respectively.

Length: 7¼ to 9 inches.

Wingspan: 9½ to 12 inches.

Distinctive Markings: Male Baltimore has full black hood; Bullock's has black crown with orange cheeks and white wing patches; orchard has black hood and chestnut feathers. Female Baltimore is drab yellow with dusky brown wings; Bullock's

is mostly yellow with gray back; orchard is dusky yellow-green and gray.

Voice: Short series of clear whistles in a varied pattern for Baltimore, short series of nasal-sounding whistles for Bullock's and high, lively warble for orchard oriole.

Habitat: Deciduous woodlands, open areas and suburbs.

Nesting: Pouchlike structure woven from plant fibers.

Diet: Beetles, bugs, caterpillars and fresh fruit.

Backyard Favorites: Fruit slices, fruit trees or shrubs and nectar feeders.

American robin

Robins

Year-Round Visitor

When you hear an American robin's light, musical *cheerily, cheerio,* it means spring is at your doorstep. As the ground thaws and worms break through the surface, robins become more active and present in your backyard. But you can find this member of the thrush family even when it's snowing, gobbling up berries from shrubs and trees. Occasionally, you may notice a robin that looks slightly uncoordinated. It may have indulged in a few too many overripe berries and is a bit tipsy!

Easy to Spot

Robins, common sights in many backyards throughout most of North America, often willingly nest in planters, on windowsills, and in other nooks and crannies around a building. In spring, look for pairs hopping around your yard. Both males and females have yellow bills and orange breasts, but the male's head is usually darker than the female's. Robins in the eastern part of the United States show white spots in the outer corners of their tails while in flight.

Raising Their Young

In a robin couple, the female builds the cuplike nest with mud as its foundation and lines it with grasses, twigs and other plant material. She typically lays four bright blue eggs and incubates them for about two weeks. Both parents feed the young, which have dark-spotted breasts rather than red ones. Robins raise three or more broods a year, especially in the southern part of the United States.

Berry Lovers

As the weather cools in fall, robins gather in flocks, sometimes up to tens of thousands, to roost together at night. They also make small migratory movements to find food. Robins eat berries year-round, so lure them to your yard with trees that hold fruit in winter such as chokecherry, hawthorn and dogwood. Watch for these classic birds in your yard, no matter what the weather is like.

WORM WHISPERER

The next time you observe an American robin in your yard, notice how they curiously tilt their heads. They do this to listen for juicy worms. Robins use both visual and auditory clues to hunt down their favorite slimy snack.

American robin

AMERICAN ROBIN
TURDUS MIGRATORIUS

Length: 10 inches.

Wingspan: 17 inches.

Distinctive Markings: Male has orange breast, black head and tail, white around eyes and on throat. Females are duller.

Voice: Loud, liquid song: *cheerily, cheer-up, cheerio.*

Habitat: Backyards, fields, farms and woods.

Nesting: Three to four pastel blue eggs in a neat, deep cup made of mud and grass.

Diet: Earthworms. Also eats insects, berries and some seeds.

Backyard Favorites: Sunflower seeds, fruit and peanut butter.

American tree sparrow

White-throated sparrow

Sparrows

It's easy to lump all of the sparrows together. After all, you can find at least 33 species of native sparrows across the country. And while their drab plumage won't sweep you off your feet the way an oriole's or bluebird's will, they're still worth your admiration and attention. They liven up the backyard scene as they hop about, pecking in the tray feeder or scratching for seeds beneath it.

Once you take a closer look at these backyard birds, you'll see that sparrows have a beauty all their own. And it's their subtle differences that make them a fun challenge for backyard birders to identify. Check out the visitors that come to your feeder with binoculars, starting with the head, both to appreciate their subtle allure and to figure out who's who.

The Crown Jewel

White-crowned sparrows may look ordinary at first glance, but their black-and-white-adorned heads, gray breasts and orange-colored bills let you know that royalty is on the premises. After all, some of these handsome birds spend their summers on the tundra or in the alpine meadows and boreal forests of Canada and Alaska. For many living in the United States, their winter appearances are considered something special.

"Over most of the country, white-crowned sparrows are winter visitors, appearing between September and April," says Emma Greig, head of Project FeederWatch at the Cornell Lab of Ornithology. "In the Northwest, they can be seen throughout the year. In many of the areas through which they migrate—the Northeast and northern Midwest—people see them pass through in spring and then again in fall."

Chip, Chip Hooray

Chipping sparrows are among the most common sparrows in North America. You know you're looking at a chipping sparrow by its chestnut cap and black eye line, though it does lose the cap and the eye line fades slightly in winter. Males and females look alike. These are some of the most low-maintenance feeder birds, because they essentially graze on whatever morsels they can find on the ground. So keep those feeders full—the sparrows greatly appreciate any leftovers that fall to the ground.

AMERICAN TREE SPARROW
SPIZELLA ARBOREA

Length: 6¾ inches.

Wingspan: 9½ inches.

Distinctive Markings: Brick red cap, white stripes above the eyes, brown striped back and a black dot in the center.

Voice: A sweet canarylike trill in spring in preparation for migration; winter call is a *teelwit* note.

Habitat: Fields, backyards, open woodland and marshes.

Nesting: On the ground in remote areas, they build a nest of grasses and stems lined with feathers.

Diet: Mostly weed seeds.

Backyard Favorite: Seed mix in a backyard feeder or on the ground.

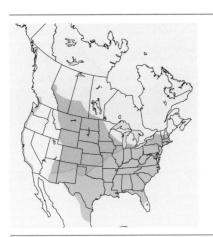

WHITE-THROATED SPARROW
ZONOTRICHIA ALBICOLLIS

Length: 6¾ inches.

Wingspan: 9 inches.

Distinctive Markings: White throat, yellow patches in front of the eyes and heads striped with black and white or tan.

Voice: *Old Sam Peabody, Peabody, Peabody* or *Oh, sweet Canada, Canada, Canada.*

Habitat: Backyard gardens, woodlands and clearings.

Nesting: Builds a nest from fine materials on or near the ground; three to six blue to green speckled eggs.

Diet: Weed seeds, fruits, flower buds and insects.

Backyard Favorites: Millet, sunflower, corn and other seeds.

Song sparrow

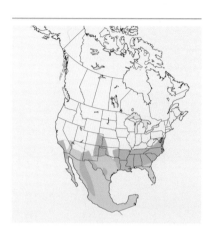

CHIPPING SPARROW
SPIZELLA PASSERINA

Length: 5 to 6 inches.

Wingspan: 8 inches.

Distinctive Markings: Rust cap, a white line above the eye and a black stripe through the eye.

Voice: A long, mechanical trill.

Habitat: Backyards, gardens and forest openings.

Nesting: Nest is loosely woven; commonly in evergreen tree.

Diet: Forages for seeds and insects.

Backyard Favorite: Small seeds.

Take a Second Look

If you think you've seen a chipping sparrow in winter, you might want to take a second look. What you may be seeing is an American tree sparrow—a plump and perky winter visitor throughout the central and northern U.S. The tree sparrow also has a rufous cap and an eyeline mark, but it summers in northern Canada and Alaska.

Sweet Singers

Another of the sparrow's charming traits: All sparrows are singers. Their styles vary from the achingly sweet song of the fox sparrow to the unexpected buzz of the grasshopper sparrow to the melancholy phrases of the white-throated. But almost all are an absolute delight to listen to.

Be sure to keep an ear out for the clear, sweet whistle of the male white-crowned sparrow (females also sing but less so) in winter—a time when many other songbirds have stopped singing. Listen for differences in the songs. This species is famous for developing regional "dialects." The singers you hear may have picked up their tunes from white-crowneds in a completely different area.

SONG SPARROW
MELOSPIZA MELODIA

Length: 6¼ inches.

Wingspan: 8¼ inches.

Distinctive Markings: Streaked with brown; side streaks join to form central breast spot. Grayish stripe over each eye.

Voice: Male song begins with *sweet, sweet, sweet* followed by shorter notes and a trill. Distinctive call note is *chimp*.

Habitat: Low, open or weedy and brushy areas.

Nesting: Well-hidden ground or low nest. Female lays three to five eggs per brood that are greenish white and heavily splotched.

Diet: Small weed and grass seeds in fall and winter; insects.

Backyard Favorites: Birdbaths and ground-level tray feeders with seeds, each surrounded by thickets or brush.

DID YOU KNOW?

Plant grasses if you want to support chipping sparrows. Native and ornamental grasses offer plenty of seed for this ground bird.

Chipping sparrow

Tufted
titmouse

DID YOU KNOW?

Tufted titmice join up with
small flocks of chickadees,
nuthatches and woodpeckers
in the winter months.

Titmice

Bridled titmouse

Black-crested titmouse

Oak titmouse

A small gray bird flits energetically through the treetops. At first glance, you might write it off as a spunky chickadee, but a closer look reveals crested head feathers and orange flanks characteristic of a tufted titmouse. These easygoing birds are prevalent year-round in the Eastern U.S. They're expert foragers that tend to spend their time in areas with large woodland trees, such as deciduous and mixed forests. More recently, populations have increased in orchards, city parks and suburbs, where they belt out their recognizable *peter-peter-peter* song. Listen for them as early as midwinter, and expect them to serenade you into the spring breeding season.

Titmice aren't attracted to artificial nesting sites as readily as some other birds, but they will use a nest box designed for bluebirds, especially if it's placed a little bit higher—perhaps 8 to 10 feet off the ground—in a shady location.

Mealtime Rituals

Focus on attracting titmice to your yard before the arrival of cooler weather. Put up feeders filled with sunflower seeds, peanuts and suet to entice these fliers. Be sure to watch for clever hoarding behavior. Titmice land at a feeder, grab one seed and fly away with it, storing it in a secret place for their winter nourishment. Stockpiles are usually within 130 feet of a feeder they visit.

When tufted titmice are ready to eat, you won't typically see them crack into a snack at a feeder, as other birds do. They grab one seed, fly to a nearby perch, hold the food with their feet, and then pound it open with their stout, round bills.

Western Species

Titmice in the West are a little more sporadic. The black-crested is found year-round in central Texas and occasionally breeds with the tufted where their ranges overlap.

The jaunty bridled titmouse, which sports bold black, white and gray field marks, calls the southern mountain ranges in Arizona and New Mexico home.

More common and with wider ranges, though, are oak and juniper titmice, which have super specific preferences when it comes to habitat. Oak titmice almost never stray from the forests of the Pacific Coast, while juniper titmice stay in the interior West to forage in dry and pinyon-juniper woodlands.

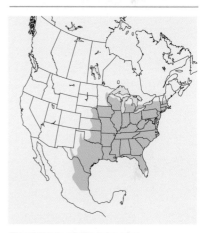

TUFTED TITMOUSE
BAEOLOPHUS BICOLOR

Length: 6½ inches.

Wingspan: 9¾ inches.

Distinctive Markings: Gray above and white below, rusty brown flanks, prominent pointed crest and large dark eyes.

Voice: Call sounds like *peto, peto, peto.*

Habitat: Deciduous woodlands, preferably in swamps and river bottoms; residential wooded areas.

Nesting: Natural cavities in trees.

Diet: Insects, berries and seeds.

Backyard Favorites: Sunflower and safflower seeds, nuts, peanut butter and suet.

Red-headed
woodpecker

Red-bellied
woodpecker

Woodpeckers

With showy and distinctive can't-miss black-and-white markings and a fun flash of red, woodpeckers are anything but wallflowers as they acrobatically forage for food around tree trunks and feeders. While there are several species of woodpecker in the United States, those identified here are the ones you're most likely to see at your backyard feeder.

Woodpeckers are energetic birds and have the appetite to prove it. Even snow, sleet and bitterly cold temperatures can't keep them away, especially if you're offering up their favorite foods: peanuts, suet, black oil sunflower seeds and peanut butter. Because most woodpeckers are a bit bigger than the average songbird, you should serve sunflower seeds in a hopper or platform feeder to allow them easy access.

Typical woodpecker features include a stiff tail to help prop their bodies up against tree trunks, and feet with two toes facing forward and two pointing backwards. That amazing foot structure helps them grasp branches and bark as they skillfully navigate up and around tree trunks, on the hunt for insects.

Red-Bellied and Beautiful

Named for the hard-to-see, faint crimson color on their undersides, red-bellied woodpeckers are widespread in the eastern half of the United States. They're more common in the southern states, but the species is on the move and the breeding range has extended north over the last century.

With zebralike stripes on their backs and wings, red-bellieds have a few look-alike relatives, such as the beautiful gila and golden-fronted woodpeckers of the Southwest.

Male red-bellied woodpeckers sport full red foreheads, caps and napes, while females have red napes and just a touch of ruby at the base of their bills. Their offspring, however, have plain, nondescript heads with a subdued red hue.

And then there's the ambiguous red belly that makes many a curious bird-watcher wonder if the person who named it suffered from poor

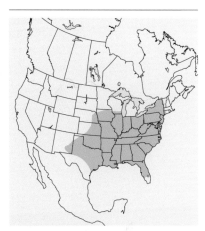

RED-HEADED WOODPECKER
MELANERPES ERYTHROCEPHALUS

Length: 9¼ inches.

Wingspan: 17 inches.

Distinctive Markings: Red feathers completely cover head and neck. Males and females look the same.

Voice: Harsh *queeah, queeah, queeah.*

Habitat: Open woodlands.

Nesting: Excavates hole in trees, posts or utility poles.

Diet: Insects, berries and nuts.

Backyard Favorites: Cracked sunflower seeds and suet.

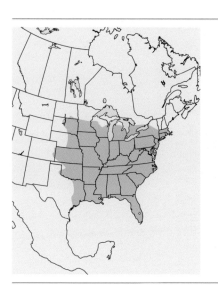

RED-BELLIED WOODPECKER
MELANERPES CAROLINUS

Length: 9¼ inches.

Wingspan: 16 inches.

Distinctive Markings: Males have a zebra-striped back, red hood and nape with a reddish tinge on bellies. Females are identical, except for red napes.

Voice: Males and females drum on trees and siding to "sing." They also have a call note that sounds like *chiv, chiv, chiv.*

Habitat: Bottomland woods, swamps, coniferous and deciduous forests, and shade trees in backyards.

Nesting: Both sexes drill a nesting cavity in a tree, utility pole or wooden building. The female lays about four or five pure white eggs, which both parents incubate.

Diet: Larvae, insects, acorns and berries.

Backyard Favorites: Medium cracked sunflower seeds on a tray feeder, suet, orange halves and sugar water.

Take a look at how small the downy on the left is compared to the hairy woodpecker on the right.

DOWNY WOODPECKER
PICOIDES PUBESCENS

Length: 6¾ inches.

Wingspan: 12 inches.

Distinctive Markings: White belly and black-and-white elsewhere; male has a small red spot on the back of its head. Resembles a small hairy woodpecker.

Voice: Both male and female "sing" in early spring by drumming on trees. Their call note is a single *tchick*.

Habitat: Open deciduous woodlands.

Nesting: Pair creates a cavity in a tree. The female lays four or five pure white eggs.

Diet: Mostly insects, but also fruit, seeds and nuts.

Backyard Favorites: Suet, bird cakes, cracked sunflower and safflower seeds.

eyesight. The name makes sense only when the light hits the stomach just so, revealing the blush-colored feathers on the underside.

Be sure to carefully listen for their exuberant, guttural *quirr quirr quirr* chatter. Unlike most bird species, both males and females vocalize throughout the year. The sound is a favorite of many backyard birders.

Downy vs. Hairy

Downy woodpeckers are among our most common and beloved backyard birds, but did you know they have a look-alike cousin: the hairy woodpecker? Telling downies apart from hairy woodpeckers can be a challenge, but once you know what to look for, it's not so tough.

Smartly patterned in black and white, with a touch of red on the males, downy woodpeckers and hairy woodpeckers look remarkably similar to each other. Both downies and hairies have black central tail feathers and white outer tail feathers, but there are a few sneaky clues to differentiate between the two. Downy woodpeckers have a few black bars or spots on their white outer tail feathers, while the outer tail feathers on the hairy are usually plain and unmarked.

The hairy woodpecker is distinctly larger than its downy cousin—about nine inches from the tip of its bill to the end of its tail. (To compare, the downy woodpecker is about 6½ inches

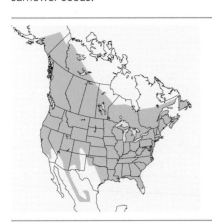

HAIRY WOODPECKER
PICOIDES VILLOSUS

Length: 9¼ inches.

Wingspan: 15 inches.

Distinctive Markings: Black-and-white checked back, with long, heavy bill and inconspicuous tuft. Females similar to males, but lack red mark on back of head.

Voice: Strong *peek* or *peech*.

Habitat: Deciduous forests.

Nesting: Pair excavates cavity. Females usually lay four white eggs.

Diet: Insects, larvae of woodborers, fruit and nuts.

Backyard Favorites: Suet, sunflower seeds, meat scraps and peanut butter.

long.) Their size difference is surprisingly hard to see, except when they're side by side, which doesn't happen often. A better way to notice the size differences is to look at the shape of their bills. The downy has a tiny, stubby beak, barely as long as the distance from the front of its head to its eye. The hairy woodpecker's bill is much longer and stronger, nearly as long as the bird's head.

You've probably heard a downy woodpecker's call: a short, friendly *pik* and a high-pitched, descending whinny. The hairy woodpecker's more attention-grabbing call is a sharp, arresting *peek*! and rather like a squeaky dog toy. Hairies also have a sharp rattle that stays at one pitch, unlike the downy woodpecker's call.

Although downy and hairy woodpeckers share some of the same habitats, downy woodpeckers are more likely to be seen in suburbs and small parks. Hairy woodpeckers generally prefer heavily forested areas with large trees.

Acorn Woodpeckers

When it comes to hoarding food, few birds compare to the acorn woodpecker. Unlike woodpeckers that tap their way into tree trunks to mow down insects, these western birds bore small, tidy holes into wood, where they store acorns and other nuts by the thousands.

In fact, just one family unit of acorn woodpeckers may create an impressive winter stockpile of up to 50,000 acorns in a single tree, called a granary. One bird stands guard against any would-be thieves as the others focus on building their impressive cache.

To make sure their treasures stay put, the birds knock each

DID YOU KNOW?
It's difficult to tell the female and male acorn woodpeckers apart. While both sexes have a red cap and a white forehead, the females have a black band separating the two.

acorn into a hole, using their beaks as makeshift mallets. If an acorn starts to loosen, one of the woodpeckers will move it to a better-fitting cavity.

Despite their name, these woodpeckers eat more than just acorns and other nuts. They also consume ants and flying insects that they snatch out of the air. Tree sap, fruit and even lizards are on the menu, too.

Acorn woodpeckers are highly social birds. They live together in groups of up to 12 or more, and they nest and often raise their broods communally. The breeding females often keep their eggs together in a shared nest, which is always inside a tree cavity made from wood chips. Multiple members help incubate the eggs.

Because they are masters at storing supplies for winter, acorn woodpeckers are resident birds,

meaning they don't typically migrate unless they run out of food. They can be seen year-round in areas with oak and pine-oak woodlands, including some suburban areas and parks.

You can attract these rowdy birds to your backyard if you live within range (western Oregon, California and the Southwest) and keep your suet and seed feeders well stocked, but be careful what you wish for.

Although the antics of acorn woodpeckers are fascinating, these birds sometimes store their food in human-made structures, from telephone poles to the sides of buildings. Your best bet for seeing these quirky woodpeckers in person is to take a walk through the woods. If you find a tree riddled with holes and hear a *waka-waka* call, always be sure to look up!

DID YOU KNOW?
House wrens are fierce competitors for nest sites. They'll even chase away much larger birds.

Wrens

The house wren is the most common wren in North America, present throughout much of the continent during summer. And yes, while their simple brown colors may be considered plain, don't disregard these diminutive backyard guests. They mostly eat insects, so you might not spot them dining at your backyard feeder very often, but sometimes they will stop by for seed or suet.

Carolina wrens, which have slightly more reddish plumage than house wrens, are year-round residents in the East.

Serious Singers

What house wrens might lack in appearance, they make up for with their bubbling songs. In fact, it's not uncommon for male house wrens to sing nine to 11 times per minute during breeding season. Listen for more of their boisterous melodies during the summer season while you're out in the backyard, visiting parks or near open woods.

Backyard Habitat

Even though wrens don't stop at feeders much, they're still a common backyard bird because they're cavity nesters. Put up a nest box, create a brush pile and grow plenty of trees and shrubs they can use for nesting. Look for wrens foraging for insects in low tree branches, shrubs and brush piles. The more places there are for insects to hide, the better the habitat is for wrens.

HOUSE WREN
TROGLODYTES AEDON

Length: 4¾ inches.
Wingspan: 6 inches.
Distinctive Markings: Dark brown above and lighter below.
Voice: The male's bubbling, chattering, repetitive song rises and then falls at the end.
Habitat: Along the edges of woodlands and yards with trees.
Nesting: Will nest in strange places—boots, car radiators and mailboxes—as well as in small birdhouses. Nest built of sticks and lined with plant fibers, feathers and rubbish.
Diet: Insects, including caterpillars.
Backyard Favorite: A small birdhouse near a tree.

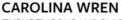

House wren

Carolina wren

CAROLINA WREN
THRYOTHORUS LUDOVICIANUS

Length: 5½ inches.
Wingspan: 7½ inches.
Distinctive Markings: Rusty brown with a white eye stripe.
Voice: Loud, piercing song that's often heard as *tea-kettle, tea-kettle, tea-kettle*.
Habitat: Brush and heavy undergrowth in forests, parks, wooded suburbs and backyard gardens.

Nesting: Builds bulky nest of grass, bark, weed stalks, feathers and other materials in tree cavities, woodpiles, sheds, flower baskets or mailboxes. Female incubates five or six pale pink spotted eggs.
Diet: Spiders and insects, plus some berries and seeds.
Backyard Favorites: Peanuts, suet and peanut butter.

CHAPTER 6

Birds
In-Depth

Get to know the fascinating world of birds—from feathers to beaks, and even where they sleep!

Sharp beak for eating meat

Fringed wing feathers for silent flight

Talons for gripping prey

This great horned owl shows how a bird's anatomy is adapted to its habitat and to its behavior.

Bird Anatomy *101*

Prepare to be impressed as you take a closer look at your backyard visitors.

WE ALL ENJOY seeing birds in our gardens. But if you asked the average person to describe a bird, the answer probably would be a quick overview of its feathers and beak, perhaps with a short imitation of its call.

When you truly look closely at a bird, though, you'll see that these creatures have fascinating anatomy that's unique in nature.

Let's consider three key areas.

Feathers

The most noticeable feature of bird anatomy is the feather. No other living group of animals on the planet has them (although some extinct ones did). And as much as feathers may resemble one another superficially, they're all different. Owls, for instance, have large flight feathers with a delicate fringe along the outer edge that allows for completely silent flight.

But there's more to feathers than flight. After all, not all birds fly, but they all have feathers. In fact, feathers most likely first evolved as a means of insulation and protection from the elements, like hair in mammals.

Birds use their feathers for communication. Males of many species sport brightly colored or ornate ones as a way to woo females. And most species can puff up their feathers to intimidate rivals or predators.

Beaks

Whether you prefer to say beaks or bills, these are as varied as feathers. Each is adapted to the kinds of food the bird eats. Cardinals and grosbeaks have heavy, blunt beaks designed to crush the shells of seeds and nuts. Robins, mockingbirds and catbirds have narrow, pointed beaks for plucking berries and catching insects. Mourning doves, quail and sparrows have short beaks for picking tiny seeds. Hawks have sharp, curved beaks for eating meat, while hummingbirds have long, narrow beaks to reach into tubular flowers for sweet nectar.

Birds also use their beaks to fend off attacks.

Feet

The bird world has a surprising diversity of feet, each shape suited to the species' survival. Ducks and other waterfowl have webbed feet to propel them through the water. Birds of prey are armed with sharp, hooked talons for catching and killing. Wading birds such as herons have wide feet to support them on sticky mud without sinking. Songbirds have delicate, grasping feet for clutching the tree branches where they perch. Woodpeckers and their relatives have zygodactyl feet—with two toes pointing forward and two backward—which allow them to cling to and move up and down tree trunks.

No matter what shape, size or color of the various features of a bird's anatomy, one thing is true: They all help birds survive. The next time you're watching birds in your yard, take a minute to notice their anatomical features and marvel at the beautiful symbiosis that every bird species has with its environment.

BIRD DINOSAURS

Not all dinosaurs went extinct—one branch of these ancient reptiles evolved into birds. We know this because modern birds share anatomical features with a group of small, carnivorous dinosaurs. They have the same kind of respiratory system, many skeletal structures in common and, yes, even feathers. Look at an ostrich or a hawk and it's easy to imagine a velociraptor, a dinosaur species that we now know was indeed feathered.

A Rainbow *of Birds*

From the bright cherry red of cardinals to the subtle violet shimmer of purple martins, birds come in jaw-dropping hues.

Male northern cardinal sits in a red horse chestnut tree

NORTHERN CARDINAL

R E D

The most popular backyard beauty dressed in scarlet is the northern cardinal. The source of the cardinal's name may not be as obvious today, but in the 1600s and 1700s it was a well-known reference to the red garments worn by cardinals of the Roman Catholic clergy. Female and juvenile northern cardinals show only a blush of the signature red on their wings, tails and crests. This species eats seed and is most comfortable on a platform feeder or eating right off the ground.

Baltimore oriole
in mulberry

ORIOLE

ORANGE

Orioles come in various shades ranging from vibrant lemon to rusty chestnut, but the boldest colors belong to Baltimore, Bullock's and hooded orioles. It's fitting that they love oranges. Attract orioles by setting out orange halves. After the birds slurp the fruit cup empty, refill it with jelly. Grape is a tried-and-true flavor, but orange marmalade works, too, and fits the happy color theme.

AMERICAN GOLDFINCH

As each summer peaks, so does the brightest yellow brilliance of the American goldfinch. In winter, the buttery hue is replaced by a brown-tinged drab tone, but in summer these little songbirds light up the landscape. Attract them practically anywhere in the country with their favorite food: thistle. Fill a mesh sock feeder with thistle seeds to draw these birds to your yard.

American goldfinch on rudbeckia

Female ruby-throated hummingbird

FEMALE HUMMINGBIRD

While the other birds of our rainbow are male, female hummingbirds are shimmering green stars. The flashy throat patches on male hummingbirds help narrow down identification, though females and young birds are tricky to confirm. In the East, any green hummingbird you see is most likely a ruby-throat, but in the Southwest, numerous and nearly identical species overlap. Wherever you are, fill sugar-water feeders with homemade nectar to attract these green gems.

THE PAINTER'S PALETTE

Red, blue, yellow and green are splashed across the male painted bunting's vibrant feathers. Females and young males sport a more subdued greenish yellow. If you live in south-central or southeastern states, set out millet seed to attract them.

JAY: JAMES PIERCE/SHUTTERSTOCK

Blue jay on crabapple

BLUE JAY

Most feather colors are created mainly by pigment, but bright blues, like those on a blue jay, are different. A unique keratin pattern allows blue light to bounce back at the viewer. This structural color comes from surfaces that scatter blue light and absorb the rest. Blue jays make their presence known in the backyard with raucous squawks. It's as though they like attention and don't take kindly to being ignored! Jays eagerly raid bird feeders and are especially fond of peanuts.

INDIGO BUNTING

Adult male indigo buntings reflect their name with brilliantly bright feathers. Looking for the classic conical bunting beak is helpful when trying to identify females and juveniles, which are cryptic brown with faint blue tones. Buntings eat both black oil sunflower seeds and thistle. If you live in the Midwest or eastern part of the U.S., serve a mix of finely chopped sunflower seed chips and thistle in a tube or sock feeder.

Indigo bunting on red crossvine

Purple martin
in flight

PURPLE MARTIN

V I O L E T

The violet-hued purple martins are entirely
aerial insectivores, so they won't stop at backyard
feeders. Martins even drink on the wing by flying
low over ponds and skimming their bills across
the surface. The secret to attracting them is to
set up multichambered nest boxes near open
areas for them to raise their young.

Creating a purple martin neighborhood is an
old practice. Precolonial Native Americans hung
up empty gourds for the birds to use. Today,
purple martins in the eastern U.S. nest almost
exclusively in birdhouses.

Beyond *Flight*

Gain a new appreciation for the power of feathers.

THE GORGEOUS red plumage of a cardinal or the vivid blue of a blue jay can make us stop in our tracks with their beauty. Feathers are among the things that make birds so special and no other creature in the animal kingdom has them. But feathers don't just look pretty—they also perform some very important jobs.

Structure

Feathers are among nature's most remarkable structures. A typical feather has a narrow shaft running through the center and a flat vane on either side. The vanes are made up of thin barbs, and each barb has tiny branches called barbules, which often have microscopic hooks along the edges. If the barbs are separated, they can be zipped together again, with the tiny hooks holding them together to form a thin but strong surface.

Underneath this outer layer, there's usually a layer of down feathers. These feathers lack the tiny hooks that hold the barbs together, so they're very soft and loose.

Thermoregulation

Thermoregulation is a bird's ability to keep itself at a comfortable temperature. Feathers act as insulation against the cold and heat. The number of feathers on a bird varies with the season, and a bird will typically have more feathers during the winter months. Birds can

Close-up of blue jay feathers

Wood duck males have bright and beautiful plumage, but they are actually quite elusive. They hide in vegetative cover alongside ponds and rivers.

FUN FEATHERED FACT

Hummingbirds beat their wings about 60 times per second, creating a soft buzzing sound.

Anna's hummingbird

Painted bunting

also fluff out their feathers to hold in even more heat. In lower temperatures, the muscles below the skin automatically contract, just as ours do when we get goose bumps. The contracting muscles raise the feathers, which creates more air space between the feathers and skin and traps warm air in the plumage.

Between the bird's skin and the outer coating of visible feathers is the layer of soft down feathers. Anyone who wears a down jacket or sleeps under a down comforter knows the insulating power of these feathers very well. Some birds take advantage of this built-in insulation and use it in their nests. Female eider ducks will pluck some of their own down feathers to line their nests, creating a cozy, insulated layer around their eggs.

Decoration

Colorful feathers are one of the reasons birds are so popular. Of course, birds don't wear those beautiful hues for us, but for each other.

Male birds with the brightest colors or fanciest plumage often have the best chance of attracting a mate and defending a nesting territory against other males.

5 BIRDS WITH IMPRESSIVE FEATHERS

SCISSOR-TAILED FLYCATCHER: Tail feathers longer than the bird's body.

SNOWY EGRET: Elegant raised plumes on the head.

RUFFED GROUSE: Impressive neck feathers when the male displays.

WOOD DUCK: Gorgeous pattern, including blue and green feathers on the male.

PAINTED BUNTING: Bright lime green, scarlet and blue feathers on males.

Owls, like this short-eared owl, can easily sneak up on prey because their feather structure dampens the sounds of flight.

Wilson's snipe

Some feathers even have decorations invisible to us. Unlike humans, most birds can see ultraviolet colors, and studies have shown that many birds have distinctive ultraviolet plumage patterns. In some species where the males and females look the same to us, they can tell each other apart by the different patterns of ultraviolet light reflected from their feathers.

Camouflage

Birds are sometimes safer if they can avoid being seen, and many have feathers with camouflage patterns, which can range from simple, drab colors to elaborate stripes and lines. A savannah sparrow, with its striped feathers, can almost

Ruffed grouse

Bald eagle

disappear in the dry grass of a field or marsh. And a ruffed grouse has feathers with a speckled, mottled pattern to disguise it in the dappled light of the forest undergrowth. Of course, that's only when it's not in display as the one above is.

Sound Production

Feathers of certain shapes, moving rapidly through the air, make noticeable sounds. Sometimes the results seem coincidental, like the whistling made by the wings of a mourning dove when it takes off. But some birds have highly modified feathers that create very distinctive notes, which they incorporate into musical aerial displays.

The American woodcock is a chunky bird that can be found in eastern forests and damp fields. On spring nights, the male performs a flight display, flying high in the air and then spiraling down with a twittering, chippering sound. Oddly enough, this twittering isn't a vocal noise—the vibrations of the wings' outer

feathers produce it. Similarly, a Wilson's snipe makes a winnowing sound with its narrow tail feathers, and hummingbirds "hum" by the rapid beating of their wings.

Sound Suppression

Conversely, the feathers of some birds are very effective at muffling sounds. Owls, which have the remarkable ability to fly with silent wingbeats, are a great example. Although most birds have large flight feathers that are strong and stiff, owls' flight feathers have soft, loose edges, deadening the sound when their wings cut through the air.

Fishing owls are the exception, though. As tropical predators that swoop down to catch fish in streams and rivers, they lack softened flight feathers—because the fish can't hear them!

The next time you admire the beautiful feathers or colors of a bird, take a closer look. You might be surprised by what you find!

How Do *Birds Fly?*

...and other questions you've always wondered about.

BIRDS ARE FASCINATING. They can fly, sing beautiful songs and travel incredible distances. But how? Not satisfied with the age-old reply, "Because that's just the way it is"? We weren't, either. So we found some of these answers from our friends at The Cornell Lab of Ornithology, excerpted from Laura Erickson's wonderful book, *The Bird Watching Answer Book.*

SPREAD YOUR WINGS

The wing shape of this roseate spoonbill allows it to soar through the air rather than flap its wings to stay in flight.

Ruby-throated hummingbird

Q How do birds fly?

Birds' wings are shaped to form an airfoil. When a bird moves forward through the air, the shape and curve of the wing cause the air to flow faster above the wing than below it. The faster air above lowers the pressure (drawing the bird upward), while the slower air below raises the pressure (pushing the bird upward). This force holding the bird up is called lift, and it requires that the bird be moving forward or facing into a fairly stiff wind.

Q Can birds smell?

Birds don't have a specialized nose but simply have nostrils, necessary for breathing and usually located near the base of the upper bill.

But some species, including several ground birds and also some North American vultures and marine species, do have fairly large olfaction (smell) centers in their brains.

Recent studies have shown that some songbirds with relatively tiny olfaction centers in their brains can smell. For example, cedar waxwings, which eat berries that can ferment and make them sick, have a better sense of smell than tree swallows, which probably can't take in the odors of flying insects as they snap and swallow them in flight.

Some homing pigeons use the sense of smell as one cue for navigating home. And some seabirds use their sense of smell to locate their nest.

Q Do birds see colors?

Yes, and they can even see some wavelengths in the light spectrum that are invisible to humans. Birds use their excellent color vision to find food, such as ripe fruits and flowers. Their colorful plumage is important in courtship. Studies have shown that when given a choice, female birds often prefer males with the most colorful feathers.

Birds can also detect polarized light that humans can't see. Experiments show that pigeons and migratory songbirds use polarized light as a cue to help them navigate in the right direction.

Q Why are bird droppings white, and do birds "go" while flying?

If you examine bird droppings closely, you'll see they're made up of two parts—brownish dark green, which is the fecal matter, and the white, which is urine.

Birds tend to release their droppings right before or during takeoff. On flights that last longer than a few minutes, they can and do release while flying.

Baltimore oriole

Snow geese

Blue-footed booby

Q Why do blue-footed boobies have blue feet?

They have large webbed feet ranging in color from pale turquoise to a deep aquamarine. Booby foot color is brightest when birds are well fed on nutritious fish—in captivity, when deprived of a good diet, the foot color grows noticeably duller within 48 hours.

Q How do birds know when to migrate?

From the time they hatch, migratory birds apparently respond instinctively, growing restless as the day length and angle of the sun change in spring and fall.

By responding to day length, birds arrive on their breeding grounds at the best average time, regardless of weather conditions wherever the bird has wintered. In fall, this restlessness helps ensure that the journey will take place while rich food resources are most likely available.

Some people assume that their feeders will entice birds to remain too long, but this restlessness ensures they do not.

Q How do birds learn their songs?

Some scientists have devoted their careers to figuring this out, species by species. Some bird songs are hardwired into a bird's brain. Virtually all flycatchers, including kingbirds and phoebes, fall into this category.

Marsh wrens imitate elements of songs they hear. Sedge wrens seem to improvise their own song repertoires. American robins share some whistles with neighbors, so they apparently learn song elements from one another. Baltimore orioles may learn their songs from their fathers and neighboring orioles during their first summer. It's possible to detect differences between songs of yearlings and older males, so orioles adjust their songs at least until they're 2 years old.

Q How do migrating birds know where to go and how to get there?

Some species, such as cranes and geese, learn their migratory routes from their parents. They follow their parents on their first flight south, and sometimes for part of the return trip north in spring, and then are on their own.

Most birds, however, cannot depend on their parents. Young hummingbirds and loons migrate days or weeks after their parents have left, and yet the young birds know which way to head, how far to go and when to stop. The more we study the intricacies of orientation and navigation, the more miraculous it seems!

Q If birds have "eagle eyes," why do they crash into windows, power lines and guy wires?

Window glass is not only clear; it's reflective. Sky and trees are mirrored in windows, and since there was no such thing as glass in the natural world for the millions of years that birds have been evolving, few wild birds have yet evolved any ability to notice it.

Unlike branches and other natural structures, power lines and guy wires are straight and relatively thin, so they apparently appear two-dimensional, making it difficult for birds to gauge their distance from one until they're crashing into it.

American robin

Q Do birds sing especially loud at dawn?

Yes, and they sing with more energy and variety. This "dawn chorus" actually starts an hour or so before dawn in spring and early summer. The chorus often begins with American robins singing a much more rapid, excited version of their daytime song. Chipping sparrows sing their songs at a frenetic pace, and many other birds sing with exceptional energy as well.

Ornithologists don't know exactly why birds sing so vigorously in the early morning. It could be that they have a lot of energy after a good night's sleep or that in the dim light, territorial competitors and prospective mates don't have much else to do but listen. Or it could be that the singing might attract potential mates that may have landed after a night of migration.

Waxwing *ID Tips*

Know what to look for the next time one of these
elegant birds touches down in your berry tree.

Thin black mask
with white outline

Brown, occasionally
ragged, short crest

Medium size with
a body length of
about 6 inches

Waxy red tips
on pointed
wing feathers

Pale yellow belly

Cedar waxwings are one
of the few bird species
that can survive on fruit
alone for several months.

Bright yellow band
on squared tail tip

A CASE OF MISTAKEN IDENTITY

Bohemian waxwings, found in the North and
Northwest, are sometimes confused for their
strikingly similar cedar waxwing cousins. A good
way to tell the two species apart is to check the wing
markings and tail base color. Bohemian waxwings
have rusty red underneath the base of their tails and
bold white wing markings in areas where the cedar
waxwings are plain gray.

Sweet *Beaks*

No matter the challenge, birds have the perfect tools for the job—right in front of their noses.

NORTHERN CARDINALS have thick beaks for cracking seeds.

ROSE-BREASTED GROSBEAKS use their cone-shaped beaks for eating sunflower seeds.

BLUE-GRAY GNATCATCHERS eat insects with their tweezerlike bills.

A BIRD'S BEAK is the most important resource it has, and every species has one solely designed for survival. Birds use beaks for just about everything: building nests, feeding their young, cleaning their feathers, defending themselves and eating (of course). But while birders have been able to pin down how each variety of beak is used, there's one answer they haven't landed on: Is it bill or is it beak?

Even around the *Birds & Blooms* office, we're not always sure if we should say beak or bill. So we asked naturalists Kenn and Kimberly Kaufman to weigh in. "Ornithologists tend to say bills; the general public tends to say beaks," they say. "One distinction that's sometimes made is that a beak is more like the hooked beak of a hawk or an owl, while bill fits better with little birds like warblers."

Whether you say beak or bill, here are some of the ways you'll spot them being used right in your own backyard.

Cracking Seeds

Fill your favorite backyard feeder with sunflower seeds and wait for birds with cone-shaped bills to swoop in for lunch. Birds like northern cardinals, rose-breasted grosbeaks, evening grosbeaks and purple finches have thick, short beaks designed for breaking open seeds with ease. The next time one lands at a feeder, grab a handy pair of binoculars and watch closely. It expertly uses its tongue to fit a seed snugly in a special groove between its upper and lower jaws. Then, crunch! The tough hull splits in two and the meat disappears into its mouth.

Not all birds of this beak type eat large seeds, though. The American goldfinch, for example, loves thistle, or Nyjer. Its small beak is perfect for tiny, tough thistle seeds. But no matter the size of the bird, from dark-eyed juncos to purple finches, cone-shaped bills are some of the strongest around.

HUMMINGBIRDS, like this Anna's, use their thin bills to catch small insects.

WHAT ARE BIRD BEAKS MADE OF?

YOUR FINGERNAILS AND BIRD BILLS HAVE SOMETHING IN COMMON: They both consist of a protein called keratin. The keratin layer over beak bone gives bills their glossy appearance. As the keratin wears down with use, a new layer forms, so the beak stays sharp and sleek.

RED-BELLIED WOODPECKERS need their chisel-like bill to drill into tree trunks.

A SHARP HOOK helps a bald eagle eat its dinner.

Sipping Nectar

A hummingbird just wouldn't be the same without its slender, tubular bill. These birds zip from feeder to feeder, slurping up nectar with their tongues the way a butterfly does with its proboscis. Hummingbirds don't have long bills simply to keep their equally long tongues contained, though. They also take full advantage of their unique beaks to catch insects such as fruit flies. A hummingbird's bill is very thin and long, which makes an excellent bug-catching tool, because it can snap open and shut in less than a hundredth of a second.

Hunting Prey

For birds that gulp down seeds and insects, being toothless doesn't pose much of a problem. But large raptors, like red-tailed hawks, bald eagles and great horned owls, survive on prey they can't necessarily swallow whole. They need the best tool for the job: sharp, hooked beaks that pierce, pluck and pull. Without this beak shape, raptors wouldn't be able to tear their meat into bite-sized, manageable pieces.

It's not just raptors that sport intimidating beaks. Shrikes are predatory songbirds that have hooked beaks to help them feed on everything from lizards and insects to small birds and mammals. They're known to kill more prey in one sitting than they can eat, and to store the leftovers for later. Vireos are mini predators, too, and use the curved hook at the end of their beaks to methodically hunt for caterpillars.

Catching Insects

Many birds rely on insects as their primary food source, so their beaks complement their bug-hunting styles. Warblers, gnatcatchers and wrens have slender, tweezerlike bills fit for plucking unsuspecting insects off leaves and tree branches with precision.

Some other species prefer hitting the bird equivalent of the drive-thru. Purple martins, nighthawks and flycatchers have wide, flattened beaks perfect for catching insects in midair. Tree swallows, in particular, are known for their air acrobatics. If you want to invite the spectacle to your yard, set up a simple nest box in spring—the same as you would for a bluebird—then get ready to see their beaks in action.

Drilling Holes

If you've watched a woodpecker hammer away at a tree, you may have wondered how it doesn't get a headache. It bores its way into trees using its strong, powerful beak with a chisel-like tip, pecking slowly and deliberately. To be able to drill holes with that much force and not come away with a concussion, a woodpecker's beak and skull has to act like the ultimate shock absorber. Its beak is covered in layers of keratin, a protein that helps the beak stand up to compressing forces, and its skull is thick and spongy, which absorbs the rest of the impact.

Spot a Red-Bellied

Use these clues to correctly ID this wide-ranging woodpecker.

Long bill for excavating nest sites and foraging for insects in tree bark

Faint red belly feathers are visible only in certain light

Four toes with claws—two face forward, two face back

Red stripe runs from forehead to nape of the neck on males (only nape is red on females)

Pale feathers cover the face and belly

Black-and-white bars on back and wings

Stiff tail feathers offer support when clinging to tree trunks

ATTRACT A RED-BELLIED with peanuts, suet and berry-producing trees, such as hawthorn.

WOODPECKER MIX-UP

Despite its straightforward name, the red-bellied woodpecker causes some confusion at bird feeders. The red belly it's named for is so faint that most people can't see it. Plus the fire-engine red head results in many calling it a red-headed woodpecker, which is actually an entirely different bird.

STEVE AND DAVE MASLOWSKI

Nocturnal species, like this nighthawk, are active at night and roost during the day.

Where Do *Birds Sleep?*

Find out where your feathered friends take shelter to catch some zzz's.

NOTHING FEELS as good as crawling into bed after a long day and nodding off for a night's rest. If you were a bird, you wouldn't need a bed, but you'd definitely need to find time in your busy schedule of feeding, avoiding predators, migrating, courting, egg laying and caring for your young to get some sleep.

Most bird species are diurnal: They're generally active during the daylight hours and sleep at night. This is the case for songbirds and hummingbirds. Nocturnal species, such as owls, common nightjars, whippoorwills and chuck-will's-widow, are active at night and roost during the day.

Taking Cover

No matter when they sleep, just catching some shut-eye can be dangerous for birds. A whole host of predators will happily make a meal of a roosting bird that doesn't wake up in time to see it coming. To avoid predators, birds rely on camouflage and sleeping quarters that are out of sight. That's why finding a bird sleeping is one of the most difficult achievements for any wildlife watcher. Even flocking birds whose strategy is safety in numbers, like blackbirds, starlings, robins or cedar waxwings, are hard to find when they're sleeping if you didn't see where they all roosted at dusk.

Not surprisingly, each species tends to sleep in the same places it finds cover from the elements, hides from predators and lays

Costa's hummingbird

Screech-owl

Mourning doves

ROOSTING BOXES

A roosting box is a man-made structure you can put up to help birds looking for a safe place to sleep. Roosting boxes look very similar to nesting boxes, but typically the entry hole is closer to the bottom, and the interior is equipped with multiple perches to accommodate several birds in one box. Bluebirds are known to use roosting boxes, especially in winter, when they can huddle together inside for warmth.

its eggs. Understory birds such as mockingbirds, thrashers and cardinals sleep in dense vegetation of shrubs, vines and small trees, while other species sleep up in the branches of canopy trees, including doves, owls, jays, crows and warblers. Cavity nesters such as woodpeckers and bluebirds sleep inside tree holes. Ground-dwelling birds like quail and short-eared owls sleep on the ground. Waterfowl often sleep floating on the surface of the water. During nesting season, parent birds will sleep on the nest. Wrens sleep just about anywhere, including old nests of other birds, tree cavities, old wasps' nests, and even pockets and folds of clothing hung out to dry.

How It's Done

Usually, a sleeping bird turns its head around over its back, tucking its beak under the shoulder feathers. Some species, such as doves, sleep with their heads facing forward, nestled between their shoulders. Birds don't tuck their heads under their wings when they sleep because they need to be able to open an eye quickly and spot danger at the slightest sound.

But migration changes things. Migratory species can't waste time getting from their wintering grounds to their summer breeding grounds, and many species migrate straight through the night. But that doesn't mean they don't sleep. Some birds have the ability to sleep on the wing by turning off one half of their brain while the other half remains active. This unihemispheric slow-wave sleep, as it's known, lets birds keep one eye open for predators while continuing to soar and flap their wings to remain in flight. It's just one more reason birds are amazing creatures.

Hummingbird *Sounds*

Learn what you should be listening for during summer.

Anna's hummingbird

Q Why does a hummingbird hum?

Because it can't remember the words!

OK, that's a pretty bad joke, but it addresses an interesting point. The humming for which hummingbirds are named isn't a vocal sound, but one created by the rapid beating of their tiny wings. This isn't the only sound hummingbirds make. Let's take a look at other sounds you might hear.

Regular Calls

All hummingbirds make short, soft call notes. These are often useful for identifying species. In the West, for example, the soft *teew* of a black-chinned hummingbird is very different from the musical *chip* of a rufous hummingbird or the thin *tic* of a Costa's hummingbird.

Aggressive Calls

Hummingbirds are amazingly feisty creatures, constantly sparring over choice flower patches and feeders. Their aerial battles are mostly just bluffing, but they pump up the effect with all kinds of chattering, squealing noises. When a large number of hummingbirds gather, most of the sounds that you hear will be these aggressive calls.

Songs

Yes, some hummingbirds do sing! The champion singer among North American hummers is the male Anna's hummingbird, which is very common along the Pacific Coast. He will sit on a high perch and sing for minutes at a time, a scratchy series of notes punctuated by a loud *tzzip, tzzip*! The one pictured at right is singing, but as you can see, it doesn't open its mouth very wide. In the desert southwest, the male Costa's

The male Anna's hummingbird is a champion singer.

hummingbird also sings, but with a thin, piercing whistle instead.

Although many kinds of tropical hummingbirds have noteworthy songs, most of those in North America aren't as accomplished as the Anna's or Costa's hummers. For example, what passes for song from the male ruby-throated hummingbird is just a monotonous series of calls, given mostly at dawn.

Wing and Tail Sounds

Many hummingbird sounds are produced by the feathers of the wings or tail vibrating against the air. The male broad-tailed hummingbird of the Rocky Mountain region has an especially impressive sound. You can always tell when an adult male broad-tail flies past, because of the high, metallic trilling of his wings.

Although the male ruby-throat's wing sounds are not as obvious, the pointed outer feathers of his wings create a high-pitched whine during his flight displays, while shorter inner feathers make a rattling sound when he changes directions.

The male Anna's hummingbird is famous for his song, but he also produces a remarkable sound with his tail feathers. His courtship display includes a zooming dive, in which he plummets toward the ground and then pulls up with a loud, explosive pop that can be heard from hundreds of yards away. Scientists used to debate whether this was a vocal sound, but studies have shown that it's the outer tail feathers vibrating at the bottom of the dive making the noise.

Listen carefully the next time you see a hummingbird. Not only will you hear that familiar hum of the wings, but you could also hear these other fun sounds.

CHAPTER 7

Birding Beyond Your Backyard

Add new species to your life list by going on an epic adventure to find feathered friends near and far from home.

Explore National Parks

Top-notch bird sightings are almost guaranteed when you plan your trip around these magnificent destinations.

SINCE THE establishment of Yellowstone National Park in 1872, the federal governments of the U.S. and Canada have preserved some of the continent's most spectacular scenery for all to enjoy. With this amazing backdrop of unique habitats, it's not surprising that our national parks are also top birding destinations. Let's explore some of the best of the best.

Big Bend National Park *Texas*

With more than 450 documented bird species, Big Bend has more recorded species than any other national park. This generous expanse of west Texas covers a wide range of habitats from the banks of the Rio Grande to the rugged Chisos Mountains.

The Colima warbler is a bird that is more common in Mexico, but a few can be seen in the mountains of Big Bend. It's the only place north of the border that the Colima warbler can be found. Other southwestern species include the hepatic tanager, painted redstart, Scott's oriole and Mexican jay. Big Bend is also a good place to look for hummingbirds, including the rare lucifer hummingbird, found more regularly here than anywhere else in the U.S.

Colima warbler
in Big Bend

Big Bend National Park

Clark's nutcracker in Grand Teton

Everglades National Park *Florida*

In this vast wetland, mangrove thickets rim freshwater sawgrass prairies, which open out into the salty Atlantic Ocean and Gulf of Mexico. It's a park best viewed from the water, even if all you have time for is an afternoon paddle. Hiking trails and boardwalks also allow visitors to get prime views of the many species of wading birds.

Look for flocks of white ibis foraging in the shallow waters, their long bills probing the mud. You can also find rare wood storks balancing awkwardly in treetops. Roseate spoonbills look unworldly with their pink feathers and spatulate bills. Anhingas sit drying their wings on nearly every available perch. Visitors can also expect to find alligators sunning themselves at water's edge, so watch where you step.

Roseate spoonbills in the Everglades

Yellowstone & Grand Teton National Parks *Wyoming*

When you stop to listen to the hoarse squawks of the Clark's nutcracker in Yellowstone and neighboring Grand Teton, you can almost imagine what it was like for the early explorers of the area.

You'll spot plenty of other creatures with the birds. A couple of favorite viewing spots are Fishing Bridge and Two Ocean Lake. From the bridge, watch for American white pelicans, river otters, or maybe even a grizzly bear looking to make a snack out of the native cutthroat trout. Another big white bird on the waters of northwest Wyoming is the trumpeter swan, often nesting on Two Ocean Lake. In winter, the swan population grows as migratory birds join the individuals that remain in the region year-round. Fires are an important part of the Yellowstone ecosystem, and it's always exciting to spot woodpeckers and fireweed in areas that were once burned over.

Great Smoky Mountains National Park

Great Smoky Mountains National Park

Tennessee and North Carolina

Tucked along the mountains, Great Smoky has more human visitors than any other national park in America. It's also a popular place for birds and critters. For plants, this is one of the most diverse places on the continent, boasting 100 native tree species and 1,500 kinds of flowering plants.

The park is at a crossroads for birds. Southern species can be spotted in the lowlands, while birds more common in the North inhabit the higher elevations. For example, both Carolina and black-capped chickadees live here. Other southern highlights include yellow-throated vireos, hooded warblers and Louisiana waterthrushes, while northern birds that are rare in other parts of the South include golden-crowned kinglets, veeries, winter wrens, and northern saw-whet owls. Other warblers seen here include the black-throated blue, blackburnian, chestnut-sided and Canada.

Acadia National Park *Maine*

This expanse of coastal Maine was the country's first eastern national park. Whether by car, carriage, bus, bike or boat, it's worth exploring fully. The scenic vistas along the rugged North Atlantic are impressive enough, but the backdrop of Acadia includes Cadillac Mountain, the highest point on the East Coast.

Nearly two dozen species of warbler have nested in Acadia. Peregrine falcons nest along the rugged cliffs of Precipice Trail, and this is also a noted raptor migration site. Waterfowl include scoters, eiders and guillemots, which congregate during the winter. Be sure to check out the Wild Gardens of Acadia, too, where the diverse plant life can be really active with birds.

SUPPORT AND SAVE

You can pay to get an annual pass to all U.S. federal recreation sites. Go to *nps.gov/findapark/passes.htm* to learn more.

Point Pelee National Park *Ontario*

One of the smallest national parks in Ontario, Point Pelee, at the southernmost tip of Canada, is of critical importance to birds. A peninsula jutting into Lake Erie, it's like an airport landing strip for many migrating species.

An impressive array of shorebirds, warblers and thrushes move through the park each year. You can also see good numbers of scarlet tanagers, blue jays and both Baltimore and orchard orioles during migration. The area hosts great movements of raptors, too. Some species, like northern harriers, osprey and peregrine falcons, will eventually fly across Lake Erie, but broad-winged, red-tailed and red-shouldered hawks tend to avoid flying over open water. They will generally follow the coast along the western shores of Lake Erie on their southern migration.

With 59 national parks in the U.S. and almost as many in Canada, you could argue that every one of them is a worthy birding destination. So get out there and explore them. You'll be rewarded with gorgeous scenery, unique habitats and some of the best birding around.

Acadia National Park

The "Birdiest" Botanical Gardens

Feathered beauty nests among the plants in bird-friendly spaces around the country.

Tohono Chul Park

BOTANICAL GARDENS are most known for their beautifully landscaped grounds and lavishly themed gardens. But did you know they are also superb places to watch birds? These gardens provide green space and water where birds can rest, feed, bathe and drink. To make these public places even more attractive to birds and bird-watchers, garden staff and volunteers are creating native gardens, erecting nesting boxes, leading nature walks and teaching classes on gardening for birds. Here are a few places where you can indulge a dual love of botanical and avian treasures together.

ARIZONA

★ Desert Botanical

★ Tohono

Desert Botanical Garden

Desert Favorites

TOHONO CHUL PARK lies within the Sonoran Desert in Tucson, Arizona. This park provides easy walking trails and vibrant botanical gardens to view some of the 140 bird species that visit the 49-acre site. A hummingbird garden attracts Costa's and Anna's hummingbirds year-round to sip nectar from salvia, desert willow and other plants. The Wildlife Garden features saguaro cacti where Gila woodpeckers build nests in spring.

The **DESERT BOTANICAL GARDEN** in Phoenix, Arizona, features a Desert Wildflower Loop Trail where you can view exhibits on wildflowers while watching hummingbirds. Greater roadrunners nest in candelabra cacti in the Ottosen Entry Garden. Bird lovers will especially enjoy the guided bird walks, which are held often at the 140-acre site.

Anna's hummingbird feeding on a cacti bloom at Desert Botanical Garden

West Coast Gardens

Established as a teaching, living plant museum, the **UNIVERSITY OF CALIFORNIA RIVERSIDE BOTANIC GARDENS** has recorded 200 bird species within four miles of trails winding through native riparian habitats and exotic gardens. In spring, hooded orioles visit the maroon blossoms of the honeybush in the South African garden. The online UCR Avian Project offers photos and details of bird species at the garden, located on the university campus.

MENDOCINO COAST BOTANICAL GARDENS in Fort Bragg, California, has attracted more than 160 species of birds to its 47 acres of coastal, marine and inland habitats. The Mendocino Coast Audubon Society leads early bird walks and walks for beginning birders.

Mendocino
★ Coast

CALIFORNIA

UC Riverside
Botanic Gardens
★

California
quail

Urban Gems

SMITHSONIAN GARDENS URBAN BIRD HABITAT in Washington, D.C., invites visitors to learn about birds that live in cities. Garden staff have repurposed a dying lacebark pine tree into a nesting, foraging and roosting spot for birds like woodpeckers. Native prairie flowers provide seeds to hungry finches and other seedeaters. Signs offer information on avian ecology and ways to create backyard habitats for birds.

AVONDALE PARK ROSE AND HABITAT GARDEN has received help from a program called the Urban Bird Habitat Initiative. The space in Birmingham, Alabama, has been upgraded with planting beds to attract birds. Volunteers also have installed a prairie garden in the Birmingham Museum of Art Prairie Habitat, where birds feast on plant seeds.

★ Huntsville Gardens

★ Avondale Park

ALABAMA

American goldfinch on purple coneflower

Gardens for Migrants

CHICAGO BOTANIC GARDEN in Glencoe, Illinois, attracts waves of migrants, including sparrows and warblers in spring and fall. Key spots in the 385-acre garden include McDonald Woods, the Sensory Garden, the Picnic Glen and the Waterfall Garden. In winter, visit feeders at the Buehler Enabling Garden to observe pine siskins, common redpolls and other hardy birds.

LONGWOOD GARDENS in Kennett Square, Pennsylvania, hosts birding tours year-round focusing on migrants, like ring-necked ducks and Northern pintails, that stop by the wetlands in March, and warblers that pass through in April and May.

Blackburnian warbler

★ Chicago Botanic Garden

ILLINOIS

PENNSYLVANIA

Longwood Gardens ★

You can see a waterfall and garden at Chicago Botanic Garden.

Eastern bluebird

Best Birding Trails

HUNTSVILLE BOTANICAL GARDENS' LEWIS BIRDING TRAIL in Huntsville, Alabama,
meanders past Little Smith Lake, an active purple martin colony, a bluebird trail and feeder stations. The purple martins return each spring and can be seen flying in and out of manufactured nest boxes and feeding their noisy young. A local birder created the trail for visitors to learn more about the birds that inhabit the garden.

FAIRCHILD TROPICAL BOTANIC GARDEN
in Coral Gables, Florida, features the James A. Kushlan Bird Walk, named after an ornithologist who leads a bird conservation program there. Go online to see a map of the two walking loops and which birds you're likely to find at various stops. For example, the map shows two places where you can find the common hill myna, native to southeastern Asia but now established in Florida. Try the annual bird festival in October, where you can join bird walks for adults and children.

The Fairchild Tropical Botanic Garden has a special bird walk.

FLORIDA

Fairchild Garden
★

Bucket List *Birds*

The *Birds & Blooms* Facebook audience shared which fliers are on their "most-wanted" lists. Here are the 10 most captivating and elusive birds, plus a few of the top places to find them.

1. Painted Bunting

HOT SPOT: Corkscrew Swamp
Sanctuary, Florida

With an unbelievable rainbow palette of feathers, male painted buntings look like something from the imagination. But despite their brilliance, they are hard to spot. Females and young males are especially tricky to see because of their greenish color. They like to skulk in overgrown fields and shrub thickets where they blend in. Painted buntings visit feeders, making that the easiest place to check them off your list. This species breeds in south central states and along the southeast coast, and a few winter in Florida.

FLORIDA

2. Whooping Crane

HOT SPOT: Wheeler National Wildlife Refuge, Alabama

Towering at a heady 5 feet, whooping cranes are the tallest birds in North America. A rare and endangered species, their numbers dwindled to just 20 or so in the 1940s. Today the population is nearly 600, including 150 birds in captivity. With breeding populations in Canada's Wood Buffalo National Park and in Wisconsin, they winter along the Texas Gulf Coast at Aransas National Wildlife Refuge and in the southeast. You might get lucky and find one at a stopover location along these routes. Resident populations are also found locally in parts of Louisiana and Florida.

ALABAMA

3. Pileated Woodpecker

HOT SPOT: Congaree National Park, South Carolina

You'd think it would be easy to spot a crow-size woodpecker, but it's not. Pileated woodpeckers are widespread, yet never abundant. Rectangular tree cavities or chuckling calls of *cuk-cuk-cuk* serve as clues to confirm their presence. They are found throughout the East, Midwest, mountains of the Pacific Northwest and across Canada but are most common in the southeastern United States. Populations of pileated woodpeckers seem to be increasing, so your chances of finding one are looking up.

SOUTH CAROLINA

MAINE

4. Atlantic Puffin

HOT SPOT: Machias Seal Island, Maine

Atlantic puffins are pelagic, spending most of the year out at sea. In summer, they nest in underground burrows along rocky northern coasts from Maine to Scandinavia. Because they are colonial nesters, finding one may mean finding hundreds. Researchers take advantage of this trait and use decoys to lure puffins to new nesting islands. Numerous boat tours and birding festivals offer puffin-viewing opportunities, making this bird a little easier to check off your bucket list.

MANITOBA

5. Snowy Owl

HOT SPOT: Churchill, Manitoba, Canada

Some are pure white and others show heavy black barring, but either way, snowy owls are striking. They nest in the northern tundra, near the Arctic Circle. Some winters they move far south of their breeding range, always sticking to open landscapes such as fields, coastal dunes and airports. Affectionately called "snowies," they are the heaviest owls and survive on small mammals and birds as large as waterfowl. Since 2013, Project Snowstorm has been tracking individual owls to learn more about the species' movement patterns.

6. Burrowing Owl

HOT SPOT: Nina Mason Pulliam
Rio Salado Audubon Center, Arizona

Looking at the burrowing owl range map, you'd think there was a mistake. It's hard to believe that a bird so widespread in the West is also found in southern Florida, but that's the case. The owls in Florida dig their own burrows, while the ones out west tend to move into prairie dog towns or burrows abandoned by badgers, ground squirrels or desert tortoises. These small owls are awake during the day more than most and are seen hunting insects and small vertebrates in the open areas they call home.

ARIZONA

7. Great Gray Owl

HOT SPOT: Sax-Zim Bog, Minnesota

A bird of the far north, the great gray owl is found in North America's boreal and high mountain western forests and across Eurasia. It takes up to seven small mammals daily to sustain these large owls. Winter is the best time to spot a great gray owl, when small numbers irrupt southward. Observers and photographers should give great grays—and other wildlife—plenty of space.

MINNESOTA

TEXAS

8. Green Jay

HOT SPOT: Quinta Mazatlan, Texas

Super common within their range, the green jay might be the easiest bucket list bird to see. The key is traveling to extreme south Texas where their range and population have slowly increased from 1966. Partners in Flight estimates about 4% of breeding pairs call the U.S. home, and the rest live in Central or South America. Nature offers no guarantees, but there's a good chance of finding so many green jays in south Texas that your friends will be green with jay envy.

OREGON

9. Acorn Woodpecker
HOT SPOT: Emigrant Lake, Oregon

Acorn woodpeckers sport bold field marks, and they are so much fun to observe. These woodpeckers live in complex social colonies and spend much of their time caching nuts. Look for a granary tree loaded with acorns pounded into the trunk and branches to find these winged jesters. In addition to the stored meals, acorn woodpeckers eat a varied diet including insects, berries, tree sap and suet. Acorn woodpeckers are found in the southwestern states and north into Oregon.

10. California Condor
HOT SPOT: Grand Canyon National Park, Arizona

With a wingspan of 9 feet or more, California condors are among the largest birds in North America. They were once nonexistent in the wild, and in 1982 all 22 known condors were brought into captivity to establish a breeding program. Now 250 remain in captivity while another 250 fly wild in California, Arizona and Utah. Recovery has been slow because females lay only one egg per nesting attempt and don't always nest every year. These scavengers are also susceptible to ingesting lead fragments, and poisoning continues to be a threat.

ARIZONA

A royal tern wades in shallow water. This large bird is found only along ocean shores on both U.S. coasts.

Birding On Island Time

Leave the bustle of the mainland behind and explore eight of the birdiest isles from Alaska to the Virgin Islands.

The sun sets over Rock Harbor at Isle Royale National Park.

Isle Royale *Michigan*

Rugged and remote, Isle Royale National Park in Lake Superior offers a wilderness adventure in the North Woods. Listen for the calls of loons. Forest birds such as the pileated woodpecker, white-throated sparrow, golden-crowned kinglet and hermit thrush thrive here. You may even be lucky enough to see moose on Isle Royale. Plan your trip for summertime; the national park shuts down for winter.

Find little blue herons, like this one, on Florida's Pelican Island.

A brown pelican's broad wings help this large bird soar above the water.

Pelican Island National Wildlife Refuge *Florida*

Tiny Pelican Island on Florida's east coast became the first National Wildlife Refuge in 1903, when President Theodore Roosevelt acted to protect birds there from hunters gathering feathers for hats. Pelican Island proper is off-limits, but the rest of the refuge, which covers more than 5,000 acres, has plenty of trails. You can get a bird's-eye view of the island from the Centennial Trail observation tower. Visitors can see great, snowy and reddish egrets. Herons also are well represented. Look for great blue, little blue and tricolored herons fishing in the shallows. Brown pelicans are year-round residents, while American white pelicans arrive for winter.

St. John Island *Virgin Islands*

St. John Island and Virgin Islands National Park provide both terrestrial and aquatic habitats. Many familiar species from the eastern United States spend the winter on the Virgin Islands, although the area is not known for its huge diversity of birdlife. Just 35 species are found year-round, but those inhabitants are spectacular. Antillean crested hummingbirds and green-throated caribs are common throughout the year. Bananaquit, the official bird of the Virgin Islands, is easily found at forest edges and in open garden areas.

Antelope Island *Utah*

It's only sometimes an island. When water levels of Utah's Great Salt Lake are low, Antelope Island becomes a peninsula. Either way, it's great for birding, especially during spring and fall migration. The 42-square-mile island is part of Antelope Island State Park, connected to the mainland by a 7-mile causeway. Pullouts allow for safe viewing of shorebirds. Look for phalaropes spinning tight circles as they feed on brine shrimp. The island's upland habitats provide a haven for birds and bison. Scan the skies for golden eagles, Swainson's hawks and short-eared owls. Chukars, partridges native to southern Eurasia, are often seen scampering through the scrubby shrubs.

A bananaquit, the official bird of the Virgin Islands, sips nectar.

Look for a chukar's bright red bill when you're birding at Antelope Island.

Forty-foot-high Arch Rock is a must-see. It's known as the symbol of Channel Islands National Park.

The only place to see island scrub-jays is Santa Cruz Island.

Santa Cruz Island *California*

Eight islands make up the Channel Islands off the Southern California coast, and five of those are protected as Channel Islands National Park. The largest, Santa Cruz Island, covers more than 96 square miles and is partly administered by The Nature Conservancy. Santa Cruz has been called a miniature California because of its vast array of habitats, including coastal beaches and two rugged mountain ranges. The island is notable for an endemic species, the island scrub-jay, which is exclusive to Santa Cruz.

Smith Island *Maryland*

The ferry ride to Smith Island provides excellent birding. Look for royal terns, osprey and brown pelicans as you cruise along Chesapeake Bay. When you get to the island, rent a kayak to explore the bays, marshes and channels. Look for lanky great blue herons and great egrets stalking a quick meal. Bikes and golf carts also are available to rent—they're the best way to get around on the island. Just a heads up: Many places accept only cash.

Prince of Wales Island *Alaska*

Located a short ferry ride or quick float plane trip away from Ketchikan, Alaska, this large island is larger than Delaware. The Tongass National Forest covers much of the land. An extensive road network covers the island and provides adventurers with miles of exploring. Birdlife is typical of the temperate rain forest found throughout southeast Alaska. Look for red-breasted sapsuckers, chestnut-backed chickadees and varied thrushes. Bald eagles and black bears are common on Prince of Wales; both are especially visible during summer's salmon runs.

Big Island *Hawaii*

The island chain of Hawaii is home to many unique bird species, especially honeycreepers such as the 'amakihi, which are exclusive to the islands. Unfortunately, the populations for many of these species are critically low. Look for these birds at Hawaii Volcanoes National Park, and try to spot the 'io (Hawaiian hawk) and 'elepaio (a monarch flycatcher). The 'apapane and 'i'iwi honeycreepers may be spotted at higher elevations as they search for their main food source, the flowers of the 'ōhi'a tree.

A bald eagle perches high in a hemlock tree that overlooks Tongass National Forest in Alaska.

Travel Tips for Nature Lovers

You don't have to be a hard-core adventurer to enjoy the great outdoors. Here's how to get the most open-air fun out of any vacation.

GETTING AWAY is about experiencing new places, scenery, climates—and more often than not, that means getting out into nature. We understand that backpacking in Yellowstone, all-day bird-watching in Costa Rica and back-to-back garden tours aren't for everyone. But there are several ways you can have a welcome encounter with nature no matter where you're going. Here are our best tips.

3+ Months Out

☐ **RESEARCH.** A simple online search for "birds in Las Vegas" or "gardens of Orlando" may turn up surprising results. There's also bound to be an Audubon Society not far from where you're going.

☐ **SET A BUDGET.** Figure out how much you can afford to spend, then set aside some money for your special nature excursion.

☐ **DON'T COUNT OUT BIG CITIES.** City parks make up nearly one-quarter of the area of San Diego, making it a city with lots to do and acre upon acre of green space. A city may be known for its restaurants, museums or nightlife, but it doesn't mean that you can't see birds, flowers or other wildlife there, too.

☐ **VISIT CITY WEBSITES.** Most have recreation listings that include parks, walking trails, nature preserves and much more. Let them spur your imagination.

☐ **GET TO KNOW THE LOCAL BIRDS.** If the area is new to you, learn about the birds of the region. Note which species you can expect to see in the season you'll be visiting.

1 Month Out

☐ **MAKE A SCHEDULE.** If the prime viewing opportunities are at dawn or dusk (as they often are for bird-watching), you'll want to be prepared.

☐ **CHECK SOCIAL MEDIA FOR LOCAL EVENTS.** You'd be hard pressed to find a county park, botanical garden or nature center that isn't on social media. Check Facebook pages and Twitter channels for events planned during your visit.

☐ **KNOW YOUR COMPANIONS.** Traveling with family? Friends? Get a good read on just how much nature they're up for. See if they'll try at least one outdoor excursion a day with you.

- [ ] **TAKE A ROAD TRIP.** Even if you're flying to your destination, you'll see more if you rent a car and get off the beaten path at least once.

- [ ] **CONSIDER CAMPING.** You might not be a camper, but try finding a campground or an area with cabins for a short stay. There really is nothing like being surrounded by nature to open your eyes and your mind.

1 Week Out

- [ ] **MAKE A LIST.** And then check it twice! You don't want to forget any important items like your field guide or binoculars.

- [ ] **CHECK THE WEATHER.** The science of forecasting has improved so much that you can get a pretty good idea of conditions 10 to 14 days in advance. While there are no guarantees, it helps to check the outlook to get a rough idea of temperatures and possible storms. On the other hand...

- [ ] **PLAN FOR A RANGE OF CONDITIONS.** Hot, cold, rainy, windy: You never know, so be prepared for surprises.

- [ ] **PACK LAYERS.** No matter where you are, if you're up before the sun, it probably will be chilly. Bring garments you can easily remove as the sun heats up later in the day.

- [ ] **CHECK EBIRD.** This website is a fantastic resource that lets you easily explore sightings by location. From *ebird.org*, go to the Explore tab. There's no better way to see what's being spotted where you are—or where you'll be.

Vacation Time

- [ ] **BE SPONTANEOUS.** Keep an eye out wherever you go—you never know when you'll see a wonderful plant or bird. Take time to smell the roses or listen to the warblers.

- [ ] **FIND A PARK.** Look for local, state and national parks and wildlife refuges. Most are free or have reasonable fees.

- [ ] **MAKE IT A GAME.** If you're traveling with kids (or even if you're not), keep a tally of the different birds or wildlife you see. It'll naturally make you more aware of all of your surroundings.

- [ ] **TALK TO THE LOCALS.** Residents of the area will likely have insider tips on what to check out next, so it's worth asking when you're at a park or garden. People are often happy to offer suggestions.

- [ ] **FIND AN EXPERT.** Talk to the park ranger or an extension employee—people who are paid to be in the know. The folks at garden centers and bird shops can be helpful, too.

Use a backpack to keep your hands free and to keep your field guide, water, camera and extra layers within easy reach.

VACATION ESSENTIALS

Don't forget these basics to enjoy the outdoors on your trip.

Binoculars

Sunscreen

Raincoat

Jacket

Sturdy shoes

Backpack

Camera

Sunglasses

CHAPTER 8

Ask the Experts

Get knowledgeable bird-watching advice from pros Kenn and Kimberly Kaufman.

SEEING ORANGE

If you spot a cedar waxwing with an orange tail tip instead of a traditional yellow one, it may have overindulged on the berries produced by a variety of honeysuckle.

Q Some cedar waxwings lack their namesake waxy red wingtips. Can this be explained by age or gender?

Bill Heban ROSSFORD, OHIO

KENN AND KIMBERLY: That's a good observation. Waxwings are named for the waxy red tips on certain wing feathers, but individuals vary in how many red tips they have. In general, males have more than females, and adults have more than young birds. An adult male cedar waxwing may have six to eight red tips, while adult females usually have five to seven. Young females often have fewer than five, and sometimes none at all. Males and females are almost identical otherwise, though the throat is more solidly black on males. The bird in your photo, with its dark gray throat and with no red on the wing, is almost certainly a female less than a year old.

Q Is it normal for house finches to drink sugar water?

Shannan Shade MARSHALL, WISCONSIN

KENN AND KIMBERLY: Although hummingbirds are the only true nectar specialists in North America, many birds sample the sweet stuff when they get the chance. Once they learn to drink from hummingbird feeders, house finches may become regular visitors. The same is true of orioles and also the verdin, a southwestern desert bird.

Other examples of surprising visitors include titmice, woodpeckers, several warblers (including Cape May, pine and orange-crowned), goldfinches, mockingbirds, chickadees, and thrashers. Aside from birds, your sugar-water feeders also may attract nectar-feeding bats (in the Southwest), squirrels, and even bears if there happen to be any in your neighborhood.

Q The managers of my apartment complex asked me to remove my feeders because they attract mice and rats. Is there anything I can do to attract birds, but not rodents?

Kathryn Bottrell HOUSTON, TEXAS

KENN AND KIMBERLY: Building managers have good reasons to prevent infestations of mice and rats, of course, and sometimes they assume feeders attract rodents even if they have no proof. If you can discuss the situation with the managers, try showing them plans for hanging feeders with baffles to prevent rodents from reaching them, and using trays under the feeders to catch any fallen seeds. Preventing seeds or debris from falling on accessible surfaces should help keep rodents away. If you can't get permission to try such a setup, you should still be able to put out a birdbath and hummingbird feeders.

FINCH INVASION

Once only found in the West, house finches were illegally sold in 1940s New York City as "Hollywood Finches." Eventually they were let loose in the city and spread from there.

HAWKS HAVE TO EAT, TOO

It's unsettling to think of your songbirds as prey, but remember that hawks, like this Cooper's, are only trying to survive.

Q. What is the best way to protect the birds at my feeders from hawks? I thought placing one next to the house, with large shrubs on each side, would be perfect, but I often find feathers there.

Sandie Davison HAMBURG, NEW YORK

KENN AND KIMBERLY: Hawks are native birds, and their predation on songbirds is a normal part of nature, but we totally understand how hard it is to think of them going after your beloved backyard birds. The situation you describe—the feeder close to the house, with large shrubs on either side—should help because it gives the birds a quick escape route. But it's important not to have shrubbery too close, since it might allow an ambush by prowling house cats or other predators. If a hawk has targeted your feeder for repeated visits, consider taking the feeder down for a few days until the hawk gets out of the habit.

Q Why would crows chase an owl? I have seen four or five crows flying after and around a barred owl, cawing and squawking, on several occasions.

Mary Leffler REYNOLDSBURG, OHIO

KENN AND KIMBERLY: Many kinds of birds will harass owls that they discover in the daytime, in a behavior called "mobbing." Even chickadees will mob little screech-owls. Crows focus on bigger targets like barred owls or great horned owls, and they will also chase hawks and eagles. No one has come up with a complete explanation for why they do this. It may serve to draw attention to these predators so they can't take smaller birds by surprise. In the case of the crows, which are intelligent and curious birds, it may be partly a tough-guy way of having fun!

Barred owls sometimes call and even hunt during the daytime.

Males sport a black mustache

Q Two years ago, northern flickers nested in my in-laws' apple tree. They spent an equal amount of time feeding and caring for the young, so we all wondered which was the female and which was the male. They returned a second year, but starlings battled with the flickers over the nesting site. How can we prevent this from happening again?

Dori Montgomery RIMERSBURG, PENNSYLVANIA

KENN AND KIMBERLY: Male and female northern flickers look very similar to each other, but the male is distinguished by his black mustache stripe. Both members of the pair are good parents, taking an equal share in incubating the eggs and feeding the young. European starlings are nonnative competitors for nest holes used by many of our native bird species. Generally more aggressive than our native cavity nesters, starlings have a negative impact on the population of many of our favorite birds. Because they are a nonnative species, starlings are not protected by law, and some people opt to remove them through a variety of methods.

Q Why do robins sometimes leave the place where they're building a nest and not return for a long time?

Lillie Wrobel DYSART, IOWA

KENN AND KIMBERLY: There's a lot of variation in how long it takes for the female robin to construct a nest. Rarely, it may take only a couple of days, but usually it's closer to a week, and it can even be up to two weeks, especially in bad weather. Sometimes the female robin stops working on the nest for a few days if there's too much rain. At other times, she may pause for the opposite reason—she needs mud for the nest's foundation and may have to wait for rain if there isn't a muddy spot nearby.

An American robin pair look after their young.

Q One cold January morning, three robins eyed the berries in my deck window boxes. I was happy to see them, but why weren't they down south?

Ralph Stanzione ENFIELD, CONNECTICUT

KENN AND KIMBERLY: While it's true that many robins migrate as the weather turns cold, some will linger throughout the winter in the North, even much farther north than Connecticut. People often think of robins as the birds that eat worms, and this begs the question: What do they eat in winter? The American robins that remain in wintry territory eat what's available, mainly berries and other fruit. So it makes sense that they'd be checking out the berries in your window boxes.

Q Our bluebird house had eggs and babies for many years. One year, there were four eggs to start, and then three were gone and the fourth had been opened. What happened?

Pauline Kelly HOMEWOOD, ALABAMA

KENN AND KIMBERLY: This sounds like the work of a house wren. While small and cute, house wrens can be hostile during nesting season. If they set up house in your yard and encounter other cavity nesters they deem too close for comfort, they'll pierce the eggs of other species and carry them off. So we have to learn to love them in spite of their behavior. The best way you can protect your bluebirds is to make sure the nest box is a fair distance away from the dense cover preferred by house wrens, and to install another box a good distance away from your existing box.

BACKYARD TIP

Attract nesting bluebirds with a nest box placed about 3 to 6 feet high in an open area.

Q I live on the Au Sable, a fast-moving river. Quite often, a great blue heron is seen fishing off my front porch. Do male and female herons look the same? Also, why do I never see a pair of them?

Marjorie Roper GRAYLING, MICHIGAN

KENN AND KIMBERLY: In great blue herons, the male and female look almost exactly alike. On average, males are a little larger with longer ornamental plumes, but these distinctions are so slight and variable that it's hard to see the difference, even when members of a pair are together. And the pair are together only when they are at the nest. That's where they do all their courtship and all their interactions around raising their young. When they fly off to find food for themselves or their young, they go separately, not together.

Q A roadrunner slept on my bathroom window ledge last winter. What do they eat in cold weather?

Ed Tate ALBUQUERQUE, NEW MEXICO

KENN AND KIMBERLY:
Roadrunners surely are the ultimate opportunistic eaters. Their diets are incredibly varied, ranging from insects and lizards to small mammals. Family groups sometimes hunt cooperatively to stalk larger prey, like rattlesnakes. In cold weather, when insects and reptiles are hard to find, roadrunners live mainly on rodents and small birds. Roadrunners show little fear of humans and have been known to eat pet food left outdoors.

Q On an early summer evening, I was sitting on the patio and saw a female ruby-throated hummingbird at some coral bells. A male appeared and they flew together, spiraling into the air about 75 feet! Is this a mating ritual?

Jenifer Junkins TORONTO, IOWA

KENN AND KIMBERLY: We wish we could say that the male was just being romantic, but it's more likely that he was trying to chase her away. Male ruby-throats are combative little guys, and when they've found a good patch of flowers, they usually respond to others of their kind by trying to chase them away. If the other hummer is a male, they may have a brief fight before one leaves. If the intruder is a female, the male may start by chasing her and then gradually shift to something that looks more like courtship displays.

BACKYARD TIP

If you have an aggressive hummingbird chasing other birds away, set up a second feeder far from the first one.

An Anna's hummingbird braves the winter.

Q Do you have any tips for keeping hummingbird nectar from freezing? We have several birds that stay all winter.

Laurie Black SALEM, OREGON

KENN AND KIMBERLY: In your area of Oregon, Anna's hummingbirds appear year-round. They seem to be among the toughest members of the family, surviving very cold weather if they get enough to eat. To keep feeders from freezing, we have experimented with hanging them next to the house and putting a heat lamp above them. It worked well when we had a wintering rufous hummingbird in Ohio. You can also bring feeders inside at night, but it's important to put them back out first thing in the morning, because the hummers need a shot of energy after a cold night.

Q I saw a hummingbird hanging upside down by one foot from my feeder. As I neared, it flew away. What happened to it?

Margaret Hocker METROPOLIS, ILLINOIS

KENN AND KIMBERLY: Hummingbirds have a bizarre way of conserving energy. Usually at night, during periods of cold and sometimes when they're perched at a feeder, hummingbirds can enter a deep, sleeplike state known as torpor, when all their body functions slow dramatically. Metabolism slows by as much as 95%, and heart rate and body temperature drop significantly. Torpor allows them to conserve precious energy and survive surprisingly low temperatures. Hummingbirds are very tough birds!

DID YOU KNOW?

If you see a hummingbird in a strange position and a sleeplike state, don't fret! It's normal.

BACKYARD TIP

White-breasted nuthatches visit feeders for sunflower seeds, suet or peanut butter mixtures.

Q It's been said that birds have no sense of smell or taste. So why do most species prefer certain seeds?

Betty Robinson WEST BRANCH, MICHIGAN

KENN AND KIMBERLY: Birds actually do have some sense of taste. It's not well developed in most species, as evidenced by the use of cayenne pepper in birdseed to discourage squirrels. The question of whether birds can smell needs more study. We do know that some have a highly developed sense of smell. Turkey vultures, for example, have a keen sense of smell, helping them locate the carrion they feed on. It's more likely that the seed-savvy birds are making selections based on what seeds suit the shape of their bill, and following their instincts for nutritional value and seed quality.

Q When should I clean out my birdhouse?

Susan Alden LENA, WISCONSIN

KENN AND KIMBERLY: Keeping birdhouses clean is an essential part of being a proper host for cavity-nesting birds, so kudos to you for asking! This is why it's important to use only nest boxes that allow you to access the interior of the box for cleaning. In terms of timing, it's important to clean out the box after the young have fledged. Many species of cavity-nesting birds have more than one brood, and so we recommend cleaning out the box after each brood. It's important to monitor the nests as well for insect infestations—ants, wasps, mice, blowflies or any other unwelcome guests that might potentially harm the nestlings.

DID YOU KNOW?

Birds may roost in a clean birdhouse at night or seek shelter from the elements.

FROM LEFT: STEVE AND DAVE MASLOWSKI; ISTOCK.COM/DOUGALL_PHOTOGRAPHY

ASK THE EXPERTS **243**

Female eastern towhee

Q Much to my surprise, after I watched some orioles eating, this scarlet tanager appeared. He ate for four days. I was patiently awaiting the female, as my bird book says she comes two weeks later. How does she find him?

Dee Genisot GILE, WISCONSIN

KENN AND KIMBERLY: You're lucky to have attracted a scarlet tanager with orange slices! Tanagers don't flock to orange treats the way orioles do. But when the first males return from the tropics in early spring, they may have trouble finding insects to eat, so they're more likely to try different things. It's true that the male scarlet tanager generally arrives earlier than the female, but the female won't come looking for him until he has established a territory in the forest. Once he has this turf, he'll sing from the treetops to attract a female and to warn other males to stay off his territory.

Q An eastern towhee has been stopping at our feeder with mourning doves and cardinals since winter. Is it common for migrating birds to hang out with nonmigrating birds?

Nancy Jenks TREMPEALEAU, WISCONSIN

KENN AND KIMBERLY: As you know, eastern towhees usually don't spend the winter as far north as Wisconsin, so this bird was out of place. In this situation—when a bird is outside its normal range—it's typical for that bird to join up with other birds that are related or have similar feeding habits. By joining a mixed flock, with more eyes watching for danger, the bird increases its own chance for survival. Since cardinals and mourning doves are seed eaters that often feed on the ground, they were probably the best company that this towhee could find.

KEEP OUT!
Hang aluminum foil strips or reflective tape to discourage woodpeckers from damaging your house.

Q Acorn woodpeckers are fun to watch, but they are eating my house and won't slow down, no matter what season! What can I do to get them to go elsewhere?

Bill Snow
BEAR VALLEY SPRINGS, CALIFORNIA

KENN AND KIMBERLY: There are several reasons acorn woodpeckers might be pecking at your house. They could be going after insects tunneling in the wood, making holes for storing acorns, or even trying to dig a hole for a nest. You may be able to scare them away temporarily by filling in and painting over the holes they've made. To discourage woodpeckers from coming back, try hanging up something that will make noise when it blows in the breeze, or hang up long strips of aluminum foil. A company called Bird-X makes a product, Irri-Tape, designed to scare birds away.

Q Bluebirds don't visit my yard, but I'd like to serve mealworms to other birds that eat them. Do you have any tips?

Reta Walker CONVERSE, INDIANA

KENN AND KIMBERLY: Many species, including bluebirds, enjoy a mealworm treat. These are available in two forms: alive and squirmy or dead and dried. We've had very little success with the dried kind, so we recommend you try live ones. Because they can (and do) escape, it's best to offer them in a glass or plastic container with a slick surface and sides at least 1 to 2 inches high. Cover the feeder in some manner to avoid drowning the mealworms when it rains. Many bird feeding stores offer special mealworm feeders as well.

Q In early spring, my oriole feeder was busy every day. Then the activity abruptly stopped. I know that when the eggs hatch, the birds stop coming to the feeder but will return. When can I expect them to come back?

Donna Wolfe GOODRICH, MICHIGAN

KENN AND KIMBERLY: You're not alone in trying to solve this mystery. With so many people feeding orioles these days, we get this question a lot. The answer is nestled in their beautifully woven hanging nest. Yep, it's about raising the kids! During the breeding season, orioles focus on more protein-rich food, foraging mostly for insects to feed their young. But once the young orioles have fledged, the parents frequently bring them to visit feeders. We suggest that you keep tabs on when they disappear, give it three to four weeks, and begin offering food again. You just might be rewarded with visits from the parents and the youngsters!

Baltimore oriole

FROM LEFT: STEVE AND DAVE MASLOWSKI, STEVE BRISHMAN/SHUTTERSTOCK, MARC DEEB

Q Do cardinals mate for life? I always see a pair together at the feeders.

Bridget Stroede
SPOONER, WISCONSIN

KENN AND KIMBERLY: The best answer would be to say that cardinals frequently mate for life—almost as often as humans do! Some pairs of cardinals do stay together all year long in their nesting territory. In other cases, the birds leave the territory and join a winter flock, but the same pair is likely to go back to the same nesting area the following spring. Some cardinal pairs do break up and look for new mates, sometimes even during the nesting season. And if one member of the pair dies, the survivor will quickly look for a new mate.

BACKYARD TIP

Sunflower seeds are a sure way to lure in a pair of northern cardinals.

Q What can I do to keep grackles from emptying my bird feeders in two days? I'd like other birds to feed from them as well.

Paul Marsteller ALEXANDRIA, PENNSYLVANIA

KENN AND KIMBERLY: If you're dealing with a large group of grackles, the good news is it's probably a migratory flock that will stay only a few days before moving on. If they linger too long, you might simply stop filling the feeders for a few days until they go. Or switch to a different type of feeder: a tube feeder for thistle (Nyjer) seed, with very small perches, will be challenging for grackles but just fine for small finches.

Q A cardinal and his mate continually fly into my windows. I've tried covering the windows, putting stickers on them and setting out a plastic owl—and nothing seems to work. What can I do?

Laurien Jeffers BUMPASS, VIRGINIA

KENN AND KIMBERLY: During the breeding season, birds become more territorial and aggressive, especially males. When they see their reflection in a window or mirror, they think it's a rival and may fixate on trying to force the "other bird" out of their territory. They'll keep going as long as they can see the reflection, even between stickers or behind a screen. Rubbing soap on the outside of the window may eliminate the reflection, but if you've exhausted all options, you might have to just be patient until the birds' hormones simmer down.

American goldfinch

Q Where do a male American goldfinch's yellow feathers go when he gets his winter plumage? Do the feathers themselves change color?

Pat Van Ryn ELKHART, INDIANA

KENN AND KIMBERLY: That's an interesting question. When goldfinches shift from their summer gold to winter brown, the old feathers don't change color; new feathers replace them. The feathers of the head and body are replaced again in spring, as the goldfinches molt into their brighter summer plumage. Actually, almost every wild bird is replacing (molting) every one of its feathers at least once a year, so it's surprising that we don't find more feathers lying around outdoors. But the feathers are molted gradually, a few at a time, so those of a small, active bird like a goldfinch will be scattered far and wide.

Q I try to serve birdseed at my second house in Maine, but the squirrels and chipmunks devour it. I've used red pepper flakes, but that didn't stop them. What can I do?

Carol Webb SAUGUS, MASSACHUSETTS

KENN AND KIMBERLY: This can be a challenge, since squirrels and chipmunks are remarkably agile and crafty. There are a number of bird feeders on the market designed to dissuade other creatures, and we've had some success with a few of them. But we finally decided that we enjoy their antics—and if you can't beat 'em, feed 'em! We offer treats that we know the squirrels love, like peanuts and corn, in a spot away from the bird feeders. If the traffic gets to be too heavy, a stricter approach is to stop feeding the birds for a while until the squirrels lose interest.

Q Even though I store my birdseed in the original bag in a covered metal garbage pail, it is infested with small black spiders. How do I prevent this?

James Castner BATAVIA, ILLINOIS

KENN AND KIMBERLY: Your bugs sound like grain weevils (*Sitophilus granarius*), common pests of grains found in birdseed. The best way to keep out these invaders is to store birdseed in metal cans with lids. Since you're already doing that, there's a good chance the weevils were in your seed when you bought it. We're often asked if it's OK to feed bug-infested seeds to birds, and the answer is no. While many birds would certainly eat them, insects in birdseed usually indicate that the seeds are old and potentially moldy. It's best to buy fresh seed from a reputable bird feeding store, and don't hesitate to ask about the quality of the seed before you buy.

MEET THE EXPERTS
Kimberly and Kenn Kaufman are the duo behind the Kaufman Field Guide series. They speak and lead bird trips all over the world.

Birdhouse Guidelines

Discover which dwellings are best for your backyard birds.

SPECIES	DIMENSIONS	HOLE	PLACEMENT	COLOR	NOTES
Eastern bluebird	5x5x8" h.	1½" centered 6" above floor	5-10' high in the open; sunny area	light earth tones	likes open areas, especially facing a field
Tree swallow	5x5x6" h.	1" centered 4" above floor	5-8' high in the open; 50-100% sun	light earth tones or gray	within 2 miles of pond or lake
Purple martin	multiple apts. 6x6x6" ea.	2⅛" centered 2¼" above floor	15-20' high in the open	white	open yard without tall trees; near water
Tufted titmouse	4x4x8" h.	1¼"	4-10' high	light earth tones	prefers to live in or near woods
Chickadee	4x4x8" h. or 5x5" base	1⅛" centered 6" above floor	4-8' high	light earth tones	small tree thicket
Nuthatch	4x4x10" h.	1¼" centered 7½" above floor	12-25' high on tree trunk	bark-covered or natural	prefers to live in or near woods
House wren	4x4x8" h. or 4x6" base	1" centered 6" above floor	5-10' high on post or hung in tree	light earth tones or white	prefers lower branches of backyard trees
Northern flicker	7x7x18" h.	2½" centered 14" above floor	8-20' high	light earth tones	put 4" of sawdust inside for nesting
Downy woodpecker	4x4x10" h.	1¼" centered 7½" above floor	12-25' high on tree trunk	simulate natural cavity	prefers own excavation; provide sawdust
Red-headed woodpecker	6x6x15" h.	2" centered 6-8" above floor	8-20' high on post or tree trunk	simulate natural cavity	needs sawdust for nesting
Wood duck	10x10x24" h.	4x3" elliptical 20" above floor	2-5' high on post over water, or 12-40' high on tree facing water	light earth tones or natural	needs 3-4" of sawdust or shavings for nesting
American kestrel	10x10x24" h.	4x3" elliptical 20" above floor	12-40' high on post or tree trunk	light earth tones or natural	needs open approach on edge of woodlot or in isolated tree
Screech-owl	10x10x24" h.	4x3" elliptical 20" above floor	2-5' high on post over water, or 12-40' high on tree	light earth tones or natural	prefers open woods or edge of woodlot

Note: With the exception of wrens and purple martins, birds do not tolerate swaying birdhouses. Birdhouses should be firmly anchored to a post, a tree or the side of a building.

Source: *Garden Birds of America* by George H. Harrison. Willow Creek Press, 1996.

Birds and Their Favorite Foods

	Nyjer (thistle) seed	Cracked corn	White proso millet	Black oil sunflower seed	Hulled sunflower seed	Beef suet	Fruit	Sugar water (nectar)*
Rose-breasted grosbeak				•	•			
Black-headed grosbeak				•	•			
Evening grosbeak		•	•	•	•			
Northern cardinal		•	•	•	•		•	
Indigo bunting	•				•			
Eastern towhee	•	•	•	•	•			
Dark-eyed junco	•	•	•	•	•			
White-crowned sparrow	•	•	•	•	•			
White-throated sparrow	•	•	•	•	•			
American tree sparrow	•	•	•		•			
Chipping sparrow	•	•	•		•			
Song sparrow	•	•	•		•			
House sparrow	•	•	•	•				
House finch	•	•	•	•	•			
Purple finch	•	•	•	•	•			
American goldfinch	•	•	•	•	•			
Pine siskin	•	•	•	•	•			
Scarlet tanager							•	•
Western tanager							•	•
Baltimore oriole							•	•
Red-winged blackbird		•		•	•			
Eastern bluebird							•	
Wood thrush							•	
American robin							•	
Gray catbird							•	
Northern mockingbird							•	
Brown thrasher							•	
Ruby-throated hummingbird								•
Anna's hummingbird								•
Broad-tailed hummingbird								•
Tufted titmouse	•			•	•	•		
Black-capped chickadee	•			•	•	•		
White-breasted nuthatch				•	•	•		
Carolina wren						•		
Cedar waxwing							•	
Woodpecker				•	•	•	•	
Scrub-jay		•		•	•	•	•	
Blue jay		•		•	•	•	•	
Mourning dove	•	•	•		•			
Northern bobwhite		•	•		•			
Ring-necked pheasant		•	•		•			
Canada goose		•						
Mallard		•						

* To make sugar water, mix 4 parts water with 1 part sugar. Boil, cool and serve. Store leftovers in the refrigerator for up to a week. Change feeder nectar every three to five days.

Source: *Garden Birds of America* by George H. Harrison. Willow Creek Press, 1996.

Native Plants Chart

Attract more birds and butterflies by including native plants in your landscape.

	COMMON NAME	SCIENTIFIC NAME	HARDINESS ZONES	FLOWER COLOR	HEIGHT	BLOOM TIME	SOIL MOISTURE
DRY SOILS AND DRY CLIMATES (15-25" ANNUAL PRECIPITATION)	Leadplant	*Amorpha canescens*	3-8	Purple	2-3'	June-July	D, M
	Butterfly weed	*Asclepias tuberosa*	3-10	Orange	2-3'	June-Aug.	D, M
	Smooth aster	*Aster laevis*	4-8	Blue	2-4'	Aug.-Oct.	D, M
	Cream false indigo	*Baptisia bracteata*	4-9	Cream	1-2'	May-June	D, M
	Purple prairie clover	*Dalea purpurea*	3-8	Purple	1-2'	July-Aug.	D, M
	Pale purple coneflower	*Echinacea pallida*	4-8	Purple	3-5'	June-July	D, M
	Prairie smoke	*Geum triflorum*	3-6	Pink	6"	May-June	D, M
	Dotted blazing star	*Liatris punctata*	3-9	Purple/Pink	1-2'	Aug.-Oct.	D, M
	Wild lupine	*Lupinus perennis*	3-8	Blue	1-2'	May-June	D
	Large-flowered beardtongue	*Penstemon grandiflorus*	3-7	Lavender	2-4'	May-June	D
	Showy goldenrod	*Solidago speciosa*	3-8	Yellow	1-3'	Aug.-Sept.	D, M
	Bird's-foot violet	*Viola pedata*	3-9	Blue	6"	Apr.-June	D
MEDIUM SOILS IN AVERAGE RAINFALL CLIMATES (25-45" ANNUAL PRECIPITATION)	Nodding pink onion	*Allium cernuum*	3-8	White/Pink	1-2'	July-Aug.	M, Mo
	New England aster	*Aster novae-angliae*	3-7	Blue/Purple	3-6'	Aug.-Sept.	M, Mo
	Blue false indigo	*Baptisia australis*	3-10	Blue	3-5'	June-July	M, Mo
	White false indigo	*Baptisia lactea*	4-9	White	3-5'	June-July	M, Mo
	Shooting star	*Dodecatheon meadia*	4-8	White/Pink	1-2'	May-June	M, Mo
	Purple coneflower	*Echinacea purpurea*	4-8	Purple	3-4'	July-Sept.	M, Mo
	Rattlesnake master	*Eryngium yuccifolium*	4-9	White	3-5'	June-Aug.	M
	Prairie blazing star	*Liatris pycnostachya*	3-9	Purple/Pink	3-5'	July-Aug.	M, Mo
	Wild quinine	*Parthenium integrifolium*	4-8	White	3-5'	June-Sept.	M, Mo
	Yellow coneflower	*Ratibida pinnata*	3-9	Yellow	3-6'	July-Sept.	M, Mo
	Royal catchfly	*Silene regia*	4-9	Red	2-4'	July-Aug.	M
	Stiff goldenrod	*Solidago rigida*	3-9	Yellow	3-5'	Aug.-Sept.	M, Mo
MOIST SOILS AND MOIST CLIMATES (45-60" ANNUAL PRECIPITATION)	Wild hyacinth	*Camassia scilloides*	4-8	White	1-2'	May-June	M, Mo
	Tall Joe Pye weed	*Eupatorium fistulosum*	4-9	Purple/Pink	5-8'	Aug.-Sept.	Mo, W
	Queen of the prairie	*Filipendula rubra*	3-6	Pink	4-5'	June-July	M, Mo
	Bottle gentian	*Gentiana andrewsii*	3-6	Blue	1-2'	Aug.-Oct.	Mo, W
	Rose mallow	*Hibiscus palustris*	4-9	Pink	3-6'	July-Sept.	Mo, W
	Dense blazing star	*Liatris spicata*	4-10	Purple/Pink	3-6'	Aug.-Sept.	Mo, W
	Cardinal flower	*Lobelia cardinalis*	3-9	Red	2-5'	July-Sept.	Mo, W
	Marsh phlox	*Phlox glaberrima*	4-8	Red/Purple	2-4'	June-July	M, Mo
	Sweet black-eyed Susan	*Rudbeckia subtomentosa*	3-9	Yellow	4-6'	Aug.-Oct.	M, Mo
	Ohio goldenrod	*Solidago ohioensis*	4-5	Yellow	3-4'	Aug.-Sept.	M, Mo
	Tall ironweed	*Vernonia altissima*	4-9	Red/Pink	5-8'	Aug.-Sept.	Mo, W
	Culver's root	*Veronicastrum virginicum*	3-8	White	3-6'	July-Aug.	M, Mo

SOIL MOISTURE KEY

D = Dry (Well-drained sandy and rocky soils), **M** = Medium (Normal garden soils such as loam, sandy loam and clay loam),
Mo = Moist (Soils that stay moist below the surface, but are not boggy; may dry out in late summer),
W = Wet (Soils that are continually moist through the growing season, subject to short periods of spring flooding).

What's Your Zone?

Find out which plants will thrive in your area.

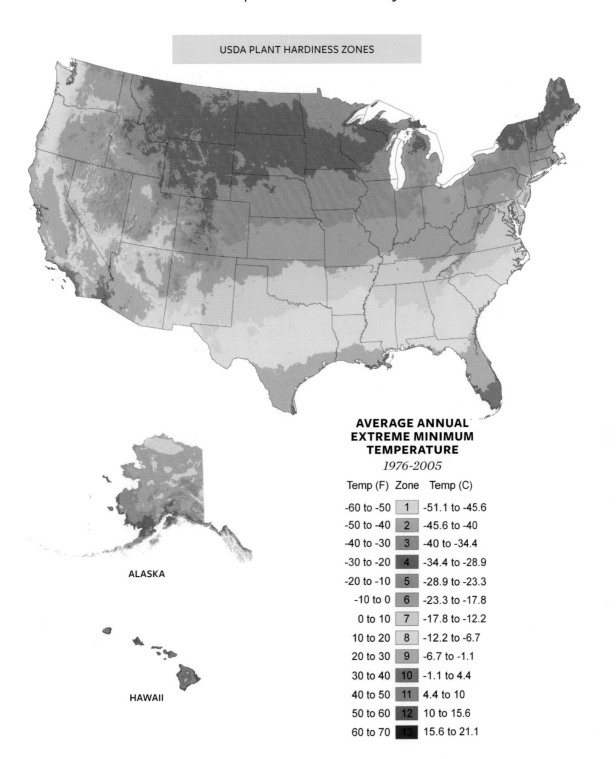

USDA PLANT HARDINESS ZONES

ALASKA

HAWAII

AVERAGE ANNUAL EXTREME MINIMUM TEMPERATURE
1976-2005

Temp (F)	Zone	Temp (C)
-60 to -50	1	-51.1 to -45.6
-50 to -40	2	-45.6 to -40
-40 to -30	3	-40 to -34.4
-30 to -20	4	-34.4 to -28.9
-20 to -10	5	-28.9 to -23.3
-10 to 0	6	-23.3 to -17.8
0 to 10	7	-17.8 to -12.2
10 to 20	8	-12.2 to -6.7
20 to 30	9	-6.7 to -1.1
30 to 40	10	-1.1 to 4.4
40 to 50	11	4.4 to 10
50 to 60	12	10 to 15.6
60 to 70	13	15.6 to 21.1

Hardiness zones reflect the average annual minimum cold temperatures for an area. If it's difficult to precisely locate your community on the map, use the interactive version on the USDA's website, *planthardiness.ars.usda.gov*. Enter your ZIP code, and your hardiness zone and average minimum winter temperature range will appear.

Red-bellied
woodpecker
in cherry tree

Birds&Blooms